THE KAI

Published by Mater Media
St. Louis, Missouri
www.matermedia.org

Editor: Ellie Toner
Cover and Interior Design: Trese Gloriod

978-1-7365190-8-0

The Kai

The Adventures of a
Mystic Martial Arts
Maintenance Man

Jamey Toner

MATER
MEDIA

Contents

For Earl—

my friend, my teacher, my brother.

And He said unto them,
"But now let whoever has a purse
take it along, and also a bag;
and let whoever has no sword sell
his cloak and buy one."

Luke 22:36

Introduction

After the machete dance—after the fire and the drums—after the blindfolds and the river—when Sensei handed us our black belts, the fruit of years of intense training, the symbols of our final and ultimate achievement—he told us only one thing: *"Now you are ready to begin."*

It was tag-end July of 2002 and I'd been walking the earth for barely a week shy of a quarter century; yet in all that time, this was the first worthy thing I had accomplished with my life. I suppose on some unspoken level I'd been hoping that if I could just stick it out, just finish one damned thing, then things would somehow get easier. I can cheerfully admit now (with a decade's worth of hindsight) that I had no logical basis whatsoever for the assumption. Always and everywhere, graduation is synonymous with commencement. Even after death, most of us will face new challenges in Purgatory. Even after Purgatory—how did St. Thérèse of Lisieux put it? "I want to spend my Heaven doing good on earth." New joys, new glories, inexhaustible, await us—but we're never just plain done.

Of course, I'd never heard of St. Thérèse at this point. And Sensei's words took the wind out of my sails. What could *I* still have to learn about life, I who had mastered the art of hitting a man with a stick? Well—virtually everything, as it turned out. As indeed I still do. And it's likely enough that my future self, ten years hence, is smacking his forehead at my naiveté just as I do at my past self now; but I have at least learned *one* thing, and I guess you can call it the thesis of this book. Like all the words of God, it's a phrase that can make wise the simple, if only we'll take the trouble to understand and apply it. It was written to a specific group of people in one time and place, for a particular purpose; but because the author had submitted himself entirely to the Holy Spirit, his words turn out to have been addressed to all people at all times, everywhere: "Therefore, whether you eat or you drink or whatsoever you do, do all to the glory of God" (1 Corinthians 10:31). By the illumination of this belief well lived, the simplest path becomes holy; without it, the grandest life is but dust and clay. And nothing in God's universe can kindle that flame if it's our own glory we're really looking for.

Now, any parish priest could've told me this. I could've found it in any missalette or catechism. The lesson underlies all the literature and philosophy of the Faith and all the lives of the saints. But although I'd been wandering the country since high school searching for Truth, it had never occurred to me to try looking for it in the Church in which I was born and raised and which even then (thank God), I had never fully abandoned. So the good Lord taught me humility—because in my own clumsy, selfish way, I was at least *trying* to knock at His door— but He used the martial arts to do it, since I wouldn't listen to anything else, and it's not even remotely figurative to say that He bashed me over the head with the moral of the story. To anyone seeking the sacred within the mundane, I hope the tale may provide some measure of inspiration; but failing that, it should at least be good for a few laughs.

ONE

Arms and the Man

PART ONE

Emptying the Tea-Cup

When I was a kid, we lived at the top of a tortuously steep hill in Vermont, where even the anthills are tortuously steep. If the valleys are to be exalted and the mountains made low, then Vermont will end up as a giant hole in the planet and my old hilltop will probably protrude from the flatlands of China. Every day after school, the bus dropped me off at the foot of that monstrosity and I got to tone my glutes all the way home, way back before anyone was comfortable talking about glutes in casual conversation. And almost every day, my big brother Pat was lurking behind the front door when I walked in.

My poor beleaguered mother, God love her, had two rambunctious boys—Chris and Pat—and was hoping for a daughter when I came along. (I was to have been a Catherine, apparently.) The elder twain of the brothers Toner are my seniors by six and five years, respectively, which is a pretty big gap for a child. Chris, the oldest, was a highly motivated fellow and was usually out doing sports or academics of one kind or another; but Pat was more laid back and was always willing to take time out of his schedule to kick the crap out of me. I believe we were just a hair on the lower side of middle class for my first twelve years or so, but Pat had somehow wrangled a deal with our parents that granted him the use of one of the two cars—which meant he was inevitably home and well-rested by the time I came toiling to the summit. Also, he was half again my size.

But please don't get the impression that I spent my formative years under a cloud of fear. I *loved* rough-housing with my brother. For one thing, it was my considered opinion that he was the coolest member of the human species; and for another, I just dug violence. My ol' pappy, he made me play Little League as a kid, and I loathed it; Chris and Pat were both all-stars. *I* wanted to do karate, but I think my folks were afraid I'd end up using it on my classmates or something, which in retrospect was probably a valid concern. So if I wanted to play ninja, it meant getting beaten up at least a little bit. And it was extraordinarily good for me: I'm a fairly small guy for a grappler, and most of my opponents are bigger than me. Thanks to Pat, I wouldn't have it any other way.

When I was thirteen and my brothers had been packed off to college, Dad took a job at the Air War College in Montgomery, Alabama, teaching military ethics. Perhaps I should mention that Chris and Pat both went on to become philosophy profes-sors—so my predilection for trying to think deep thoughts is easily traceable. But also, Mom had instilled in me a deep, deep love of Tolkien (which, unfortunately, Dad never shared), and I was always possessed by the idea of being a wanderer—to wear a sword instead of a walking stick. So I missed Vermont, and I've always found my way back there again in my travels, but I came to love Alabama as well. In Chesterton's words, "Every adventure is only an inconvenience rightly considered." And during the inconvenience of making new friends for the first time since I was out of swaddling clothes, I met *Domingo*.

Whatever they put in the water down there, it grows big kids. Almost every guy in my grade was significantly larger than I was. In fact—this is odd—it never struck me till I started writing this paragraph, but I guess it was sort of like being a hobbit among the Big Folk. Well, not quite that bad. As an adult, I clock in at 5'11" and 170 pounds, so I'm not tiny; but it sort of depends on whom you're comparing yourself to. In any case, Domingo was a good deal bigger than me and turned out to share my passion for the grappling arts. His parents were quite a bit more (let's see, how shall I—ah, yes) *clement* than mine, so we spent most of our time at his place. A lot of our sparring happened out on the lawn, but impromptu sessions broke out indoors pretty frequently as well. I actually put both feet through one of the walls once, trying to use it for leverage. Man, *good times*.

We were sixteen years old (1993) when the first Ultimate Fighting Championship came out on Pay-Per-View. In these fallen days, the UFC has become little more than kick-boxing with a longer legal clinch time; back then, there were no rounds, no time limits, practically no rules (although I believe biting may have been explicitly prohibited), and, above all, no weight divisions. Of the UFC's wider ramifications in the martial arts there will be more to say later; for now it's enough to note that Royce Gracie became my absolute hero. Here was a guy hardly any larger than myself, taking on two- and three-hundred-pound world-class martial artists of every discipline under the sun, and just *eating* them. Domingo and I spent endless hours dissecting his techniques and trying to maim each other with them.

A year or so later, when Royce's star was still in the ascendant, the Gracie clan released a series of tapes on Brazilian Jiu-Jutsu. I'm sure they made obscene amounts of money; but as Domingo had immediately predicted, those tapes marked the dawn of their downfall. Once their enemies began to learn their secrets, the weaknesses of BJJ (and let's not fool ourselves: every martial art has its weaknesses) became known and quickly exploited. Not to put too fine a point on it, Royce was defensive to a fault, waiting for his opponent to over-commit and then capitalizing; and by the UFC 5, Ken Shamrock had devised the world's most excruciatingly boring counter-strategy. I'll never forget that match—I was just getting up to go to the bathroom after guzzling down liters of Dr. Pepper during the opening fights, when suddenly they announced the battle royale. I couldn't miss even a moment of this clash of titans! So I sat there on Domingo's couch with my legs crossed in torment while the two of them just laid there on the mat, doing absolutely nothing, for thirty-five minutes straight. The most exciting part of the match was the poor ref hopping around and practically begging for someone to make a move, *any* move. It was the first draw in the UFC's short history, and the end of BJJ's legend of invincibility.

But I didn't lose my faith in grappling. I simply concluded that I'd have to learn some new tricks. I graduated in '95 and enrolled at the University of Alabama; and there I embarked on a very strange road. Over the course of the next four years, I flitted through the military and the monastery, jobs and jail, and penniless drifting through much of the lower 48. Some of the tale is interesting in its own right, and in any case it's all relevant—so don't worry, it'll be told in its proper place. For now, we're going to jump ahead again. They say that when the student is ready, a master will appear. It was in the closing months of the millennium that I at last found mine.

Growing up with much older brothers, I'd always been closer with my cousin Josh, who's only a year shy of my own age. We used to spend summers on our grandparents' farm in Massachusetts, slaying hordes of dragons and aliens with our wiffle-ball bats of justice. Late in '99, when he was studying history at

Jotun State College in Vermont, I came up to visit for a few weeks. He'd recently broken up with his girlfriend, Donna, and she was now dating a new guy. Donna and I had become friends during my last visit to Jotun, and so it was that she introduced me to her new boyfriend, the man who was to become my teacher. He was a quiet guy, a chef at a local restaurant, my own age and a fellow red-head (indeed, we've occasionally been mistaken for brothers). When I learned that he held a first-degree black belt in kenpo-jujitsu (KJJ), I instantly asked him for a match.

Now, at this point in my life, it had been quite some time since I had lost. I wasn't incredible on my feet, but I'd always had a talent for groundwork, and I'd been honing it for years against anyone who would roll with me, all across America. I had a respectable level of skill for an autodidact—but my ego had grown with it, and ultimately surpassed it. Worst of all, I had fallen into the infinitely silly trap of valuing victories for their own sake: as if it mattered in the scale of the cosmos which participant in a friendly match tapped out first. The *sole* purpose of such bouts is to grow in experience, not to "beat" your training partner. Indeed, the one who loses the match typically learns more than the winner, so in a very real sense the last becomes the first. But in my shallow little pea brain, I hadn't yet grasped this basic and obvious truth.

Thank God, Sensei trounced me. But I took it graciously enough, and he was impressed by how well I'd done with no formal study; so he invited me to his dojo for a class. At this time, Josh wasn't yet interested in the arts, but our friend Lane came along with me. There we met a few of Sensei's students, including his cousin Tommy, who was to become like a brother to me and Josh. There too we first heard that critical phrase: "Empty your tea-cup."

Human beings, of course, are born to immortality. C.S. Lewis says the fact is sufficiently demonstrated by our never-ending *astonishment* at the passage of time. (Dear God, has it really been fourteen years since that first match with Sensei?) And as such we have an intrinsic ability to perceive eternal truths when we encounter them—as long as we haven't fogged our senses too dreadfully with sin. No one could possibly have foreseen the Incarnation; but the Lord gave hints to the world beforehand, luminous flotsam of the Fall, fragments whose whole was not yet seen. Philosophy, myth, poetry, the warrior ethic, and to the Hebrews, our fathers, the Law. Also He gave us the gigantic mystery of Zen, which the Christian West is forever trying and failing to assimilate. Again, there will be more to say of this later when we come to speak of qi. For now I simply pass on what was passed on to me.

A young man who thought himself wise came to the house of an ancient master to ask him for a lesson. The master invited him in and offered him tea, and when the young man accepted, placed an already full cup in front of him. "Here is your tea," he said then, and began to pour the scalding liquid from the pot into the overflowing cup. The young man jumped up and exclaimed, "Master, the cup is already full!" And the master smiled and replied, "Then how can I fill it? First, you must empty your cup."

This koan, like any great truth, transcends culture altogether. The Greeks teach the same precept, calling it *kenosis*. Jackie Chan teaches it in The *Forbidden Kingdom*. St. Paul teaches us that even Jesus emptied Himself, taking the form of a slave (Philippians 2:7). When I first heard it, I had no immediate sense of epiphany; but over the next few weeks, as full of myself as I was, it did slowly begin to sink in. I didn't really want to learn, so much as I wished that I already knew—but I did have just enough sense to know that I *didn't* know. In the old story, the Oracle proclaimed Socrates the wisest man in Athens, not despite but precisely because of the fact that he professed to know nothing. I was a far cry from being the wisest man in Jotun. But at least I was willing to imitate the sage by asking questions and listening to the answers. Our dear Lord always comes as a thief in the night, but we tend to forget that that phrase doesn't necessarily imply stealth. Sometimes, if we open our hearts just the tiniest crack, He'll kick in the front door and take the house by storm. And thank God for His crazy, tempestuous mercy! The process, however, is every bit as painful and terrifying as it sounds.

The Returning Cousin Test

You might have noticed that we spell "jujitsu" differently from the Brazilians. That's because their rendering is closer to the original Japanese, whereas ours has been Americanized. The name means "the gentle art," which is really rather funny when you consider some of the ghastly things a practitioner can do to the human body; but, as I said before, much depends on your standards of comparison. The art was originally taught to the samurai, along with a primordial kenpo, in case they happened to find themselves fighting without weapons for whatever reason. Now, *kenpo* means something like "law of the fist" (not to be confused with *kendo*, the way of the sword), and jujitsu actually does seem reasonably mild by contrast. A good grappler at least has the option of subduing an enemy without doing him any permanent damage—although I can't imagine anyone exercising that option on a medieval battlefield—but kenpo takes a hideous merriment in smashing the organs, joints, and face beyond all reclamation.

The advantage of jujitsu in that older context was that throws and locks were often more effective against an armored foe than kicks or punches; but in the modern day, the striking and grappling arts eventually drifted apart. Judo and aikido, focusing more on throws and joint manipulation than chokes and limb destruction, became popular; jujitsu languished. But then the Gracies got a hold of it, extrapolated its core principles, and stream-lined it into a whole new style—basically doing what Bruce Lee had done for kung-fu in creating Jeet Kune Do. And Master Montalban of Connecticut, my sensei's sensei, re-fused the long-polarized disciplines of stand-up and ground-based combat, and created his own kenpo-jujitsu. Oh, and also—well, maybe that's enough martial elucidation for right now. We'll come back to KJJ's little trump card later on.

Let me fill in a couple of blanks before proceeding. In December of '97, about halfway through my twentieth year, I came back to Montgomery from a cross-country hitch-hike and got arrested. My parents were out of town, visiting Chris or Pat for Christmas, if I recall correctly, and I was wandering the streets sometime in the small hours. Evidently I looked suspicious enough for two officers to pull up and start questioning me, and evidently my obvious homelessness was odious enough for them to frisk me and discover my pocket knife. It was only a three-inch folder, nothing too ominous, but it *was* technically a concealed weapon by local ordinances. Even way back then I always addressed cops as "sir" and tried to be courteous to them; without cops and courtesy, there wouldn't be much civilization, as is clear enough from the mere fact that the words *polite* and *police* both derive from *polis*, or "the City." Also, they're human and they take enough crap in the course of their job that some basic respect goes a long way towards mollifying them (funny how often Christian charity and common sense coincide). Almost all the cops I've met in my travels have been extremely nice to me.

But not these guys. Before you could say "Jack Robinson"—I mean, if you had the sudden urge to say "Jack Robinson" for some reason—they'd cuffed me, tossed me in the cruiser, and dumped me in a holding cell with about twenty other guys. I was offered a phone call, but there was no one in particular for me to contact so I just hung out in the cell. I remember feeling very stoic about the whole thing; it wasn't as if I had anything pressing to do in the world outside, after all. I was in there two or three days, and I witnessed one fight—the second serious fight I'd seen up to that point. It confirmed once again what Domingo had always said: untrained people usually have no concept of the jab, they simply throw haymakers. Ninety percent of the swings glance off the other guy's shoulders or go wide altogether. These fellows got broken up pretty quickly.

Anyway, Mom and Dad got back to town and got wind of my predicament somehow; I think the authorities left a message on their machine because their address was still on my license. So they came and got me, and the state turned me loose; apparently my captors hadn't actually bothered to charge me with anything, though I believe the arrest is still on my record. For the next few months I lived with my folks again, holding down a normal job (on the stock crew at a nearby super-market), and they even bought me a car to help me try and re-construct my life. (It was especially kind, considering that Dad and I had almost killed each other a few months earlier.) That car, I named Dave: a grey '87 Honda Civic, and my truest companion for the next two years.

In the summer of '98, my brother Pat got married to a very nice young lady called Shannon up in Vermont, and the Toners were once again gathered in a dire quorum. Josh came to the wedding as well, and it was our first meeting in about a year. Now, I had agreed to help Pat and Shannon move to Steuben-ville, Ohio after their honeymoon so Pat could attend Fran-ciscan University; so I was at a loose end for a week or so until they got back. That being the case, Josh offered to take me to Jotun and show me around, and I agreed. It was my first visit to that fateful town.

I don't even remember whom he was dating on that occa-sion. There were like, what?—three or four different girls during this time that sort of took turns messing with his heart and head, and he broke up and re-united with at least two of them at least once or twice each. Point is, I now had a vehicle (which doubled as a home) and a good deal of money I'd saved up, so I was forever peregrinating about the realm; and I liked the denizens of Jotun so much that I came back to visit often—starting only a few weeks after my initial visit, once the newlyweds had gotten settled in Steuby. And already the man was dating someone else. It's a literal fact that every time I came back to town, he was either freshly broken up or freshly attached to somebody new. By the time I met Sensei, Josh and I had developed what we called the Returning Cousin Test. Put briefly, we decreed that if I should ever depart from Vermont and return to find him still dating the same girl—he'd marry her.

Shortly before year's end, I decided to bounce back down to visit Domingo in Tuscaloosa. Around this time, he was becoming sort of a casual beer connoisseur (he now lives in Colorado, and took me to my first beer fest there in '05), but 'Bama was notoriously weak on micro-brews; you could pretty much drink Bud or Miller, or go live in Canada with the Commies. So I stocked Dave's trunk with as much of Vermont's finest as I could fit in there: Longtrail, Catamount, Woodchuck, and of course the now-national Magic Hat. Honestly, I'm not completely sure it was legal for me to transport that much alcohol across state lines, but what the hey. We had a good few nights. Also, having recently both turned twenty-one (we have almost the same birthday), we decided to celebrate in the most enlightened way possible, and drove ourselves to Las Vegas in Domingo's new car. It was a fun trip; we took turns driving, and Pantera (that's a heavy metal band from the '90s) literally saved our lives when I almost fell asleep at the wheel during a slow part of the tape, only to be jarred back to consciousness when they started screaming again. I actually won $500 on roulette, and have never played since—although we returned there in '07 when the big D. got married.

The rest of '98 and most of '99 consisted mainly of me driving randomly around the country and working occasional jobs—an Arby's here, a Kroger's there, a sock factory in between—up until my first meeting with Sensei. (At the time, I was suffering from a crippling incapacity to commit myself to anything, or even to stay in one place long enough to perceive the necessity of committing: of putting down a root or two in order to blossom and grow.) After that, I left Jotun one last time, heading south with the intention of spending New Year's Eve in New Orleans. I didn't explicitly admit this to myself, but I was kind of hoping to be present at some manner of homicidal voodoo uprising so I could fist-fight with the powers of darkness. (You'll no doubt recall the rumors of a Y2K apocalypse at the time.) As it turned out, however, Dave began developing engine trouble, so I ended up attending Midnight Mass with my parents in Montgomery as we entered 2000 A.D. One could do worse.

I spent another couple of months down south, living in Dave and mostly hanging with the T-town crowd. We played a lot of video games. Drank a lot. I used my friend Dan's clothing iron to try to re-constitute a slice of pizza whose crust had gotten wet. (What? It was worth a try.) Lost a grappling match to a guy called Matt, who used a technique I hadn't seen before—essentially a triangle choke with the arms instead of the legs—which I liked so much that it became one of my signature moves for awhile. The real highlight of the period was the U of A winning a crucial football game (against Florida, maybe?—the details are a tad fuzzy now). We were all in Domingo's apartment, and our boys pulled out the win with a last-minute Hail Mary touchdown (I love that phrase), and we all jumped up screaming and ran out into the street—only to see that every door up and down the block was opening to spill forth its ecstatic residents as well. That night the whole *town* was one giant fiesta; I've never seen so many friendly drunks in one place. I remember finding myself practicing kip-ups in the middle of the road and having a cop car screech to a halt bare feet from my skull. The officer got out—I got up, shame-facedly anticipating a clubbing at the very least—he looked at me, shook his head, and said, "Son—get out of the street"—and I said, "Yes, sir," and got out of the street.

Back up in Jotun, Lane and I had developed a friendly grappling rivalry, and before I left he made me promise to return by St. Patrick's Day at the latest. So, when March came around, I started making my way back north. Dave was finally dying by this time, and I was almost entirely out of money, so the trek was arduous. It was late on the very evening of St. Paddy's when I made it back to town, and there I was to stay for what, at that point in my life, seemed like a very long time indeed.

Alas for Dave! He sat on a back road for over a year until some neighborhood vandals—we never found out who—set fire to him in '01. But it was a worthy end, a Viking funeral; better, perhaps, than moldering in a scrap-yard somewhere. Peace to his ashes!

On my arrival, I discovered that no candidate for the Returning Cousin Test had yet emerged. Josh had just broken up with a certain Mindy, leaving him in a rough place emotionally. It was his last semester at Jotun State and he was weary of life. I didn't know what to do for the guy, especially since I myself hadn't yet experienced romantic heartbreak and couldn't fully relate. I'd suggested to him on previous visits that he look into the arts, if only for stress-relief, but he'd never shown any desire to do so. In the end, he acted entirely on his own initiative; and as we later discovered, he thereby saved the Kai.

It turned out that Sensei too was losing his joy in life, and particularly in the martial arts. He'd recently broken up with Donna, his students had all drifted away, and his own master back in Connecticut was (to say the least) unsupportive. Master Montalban's part in this tale is mercifully brief but, sadly, almost all bad. Lane had been too busy to find Sensei for class, and I'd been out of town; and when I got in touch with Sensei on my own, he seemed unenthusiastic, and I didn't press the matter. It was Josh who called him up one day and confessed that he was falling apart and needed something in his life; considering that the unresolved weirdness of their both loving the same girl still lay between them, it seems to me that it took substantial heart for both of them to enter the student-teacher relationship.

At this time, Josh, Lane, and our friends, Topper and Rob, were all living in a rented house off-campus, which we simply called the House. Upon returning to town, I'd gotten a job at a nearby store and moved into the House as well. And one afternoon in late March, Josh came home with a strange new energy and a strange new peace. He told me he'd gotten in touch with Sensei, and that Sensei had taken him up to the empty soccer fields and started teaching him kata.

Kata! It's the foundation of everything we do. The choreographed execution of moves—slow and meditative as in tai chi, or explosive as in tae kwon do—the teaching of the body and mind to move as one. At the end of the day, it's the difference between a martial artist and a brawler. From the latter, you'll inevitably hear the objection, "You can't use katas in a fight." Why, no—no, you can't—that's a very telling point, thanks for the memo. Come to think of it, you can't use push-ups in a fight either, can you? You can't lift weights, or do jumping jacks or crunches, or go for a jog or a swim, in the middle of a fight. I suppose by the prevailing logic we should therefore do none of those things either.

Josh's excitement got me excited again—and having excited students got Sensei excited again. We tracked down his cousin

Tommy, who had also been losing interest (T. was only eighteen at this point and not yet out of high school), and the four of us became the indissoluble core of something new. When you hear the word *kai* in America, it generally refers to a martial arts group or school—which we were—but the word really means "family." And, before long, we were that too.

Quest for a Quest

I've always jokingly attributed my wanderlust to an early exposure to *The Hobbit*; but, the truth is, such things are inborn. If Bilbo hadn't catalyzed it, something else would have. As a kid, I was constantly getting in trouble for poking around in boiler rooms, climbing over fences, investigating ruins. I just wanted to see what *else* there was, beyond the things put in front of me. And, as with anything else, that impulse can be a virtue— as long as it's regulated by reason and conscience. Accepting that regulation, the submission to legitimate authority took me decades, and I'm still kind of working on it. One of jujitsu's fundamental principles is the diminishing circle: not merely bending the opponent's joint but *spiraling* it, to maximize the damage done. But while it may occasionally be necessary to do this to an enemy's knee or shoulder, it's hardly the thing to do to one's own life; and we can only go in circles, in this bent world, unless we follow in the footsteps of a Master.

It was April of '97 when Dad and I had our big showdown.

We didn't quite come to blows, for which I'm now thankful; at least I can say I never hit my old man. But I'd recently done something of which I didn't yet have the grace to be ashamed, though I'm ashamed of it now—and when I went to visit my parents not long afterward, the discussion of my shortcomings got heated fast. Dad's mellowed a lot over the years; back in the days of my long-vanished youth, he was a pretty intense guy. Awhile back I bumped into an old friend I hadn't seen since we were kids, and one of the first things he asked me was, "Does your dad still sneeze the same way?" I'd never thought about it before—the shuddering crimson-faced roar seemed normal to me—but yes, even sneezing was an intense affair for my pappy, and apparently it terrified a few of my friends the first time they witnessed it. So you can well imagine the ruinous paternal visage turned upon me when he *really* got mad.

What was it that I'd done? Well... We're not quite there yet. I'm leading up to it slowly in the hopes, O reader, of giving you more time to develop affection for your humble narrator before I have to relate the two things of which I'm least proud. But rest assured: like they say in the Conan movies, that story too shall be told.

At any rate, we finished our nose-to-nose shouting match and I stormed out of the house, and thereupon commenced long months of hitching, sleeping in bushes, and scrounging for scraps. I've often relapsed into vagrancy in the years since then, and there are a few aspects of the life that have never lost their adventurous aura for me. When I read *All Quiet on the Western Front* as a boy, my favorite part was the scene where they come upon an abandoned village that's being shelled and they ransack the place and hold a feast in the middle of the bombardment. The smallest comforts, such as we don't normally even notice, become war trophies when they're snatched out of penury. An unlocked hotel broom closet on a cold night—an unspoiled bag of Munchkins in a Dunkin Donuts dumpster—a pile of empty beer cans in a state with return-for-deposit law. The homeless experience as a whole has rather lost its romance for me by now, but back then it was all fresh and dew-bespangled madness. I soon learned the many little tricks and knacks of the, well, tradelessness. Carry Clorox Wipes for a quick shower. Check under bridges; we leave each other blankets. Use library bathrooms, they're cleaner. Stay shaven so you don't *look* homeless.

I also got in my first two fights during this period, both with old perverts who propositioned me a bit too forcefully in dark places. One of them I caught with a kick and he jumped back, reached into his jacket, and started shouting, "I'ma blow your head off!" To this day I'm convinced that he was bluffing—otherwise why not produce the gun instead of yelling about it?—but I played it safe and ran like hell. The other guy I actually choked out. (If you're not familiar with the phrase, don't be alarmed—it's just a sleeper hold. You wake up disoriented after a minute or two and you're fine, no damage done.) I have to admit it was validating. No matter how much practice you've had, it's a scary, scary thing when you really have to use it.

In time's fullness I made my way to California. As Providence would have it, a group of Russian Orthodox monks was holding a youth conference in the coastal town of Eureka, inside an old lighthouse. And here's the cool part: when I introduced myself to the abbot, Fr. Herman of Platina, he knew who I was! Two years earlier, I'd entered a national essay contest held by the *Orthodox Word* news magazine and won second place, and the padre somehow happened to remember me. *That* was gratifying, folks.

So I stuck around for the two-day conference (they put a bunch of us up in a camper), and it was well worth the trip. I met a young monk who had known the guys in Green Day before they made it big. When he got up to address the meeting, the previous speaker had just been holding forth on the cultural ills of rock and roll, and the younger guy somewhat sheepishly informed us that he was going to be singing us a little Christian rock song he'd written, and performing his own guitar accompaniment. Probably should've coordinated the talks beforehand, I rather thought. I also met an old monk with whom I spent about ten minutes—I swear this is true—talking about *Wolverine*. And remember, this was way before all the comic books got made into movies, back when only dorks knew about this stuff and dorkiness wasn't yet the new hip. Yet here's this robed, bearded hierophant in his fifties, gravely comparing the ol' Canucklehead to Allan Quartermain and Elric of Melniboné. Kind of surreal. The talk that really stuck with me was from a Russian monk who'd been in the Soviet Union and witnessed some of the persecutions of Christian believers. "Horrific" doesn't even touch it. But for me, the true highlight of the event was finding a long bungee cord during one of the lunch breaks, staked to the ground at the cliff's edge overlooking the sea. I imagine it was there to enable watchers to get down to the surf quickly if they had to, or something; but I climbed about halfway down, used the cord to hold myself perpendicular to the cliff-face, and then just ran back and forth above the Pacific for about a quarter of an hour. It doesn't sound too spectacular, I guess, but it's still one of my favorite memories.

After being respectable for a couple of days—and this is pretty much the story of my life—I went right back to being an ass. From Eureka, the monks returned to their cloister in the northern mountains of Platina, high among the redwoods, and I begged leave to tag along. See, I had developed this idea that I could spend a few weeks as a monk and—you know—attain enlightenment. 'Cause that's how it works, right? They gave me a day or two to settle in and acquaint myself with the *skete* (that's their word for "monastery"—I've never checked, but I assume it comes from the same root as *ascetic*), and then they threw me in the scullery. It would be years before I came across St. Teresa of Avila's calm, wise maxim, "God walks among the pots and pans." At the time, washing dishes seemed a tyrannous distraction from my moonlit levitation attempts. Who did I *think* was going to do the stupid dishes? I didn't think, is the long and short of it. And I hadn't yet been taught (or if I had, I hadn't retained it) that an act—any act—becomes holy exactly insofar as it is offered to Christ. Whether you eat or you drink or whatsoever you do—

I lasted at the *skete* less than a week. After that I drifted back east to visit Domingo as his fall semester got underway. During that visit, I got drunk for the very first time. I was already twenty, which I know is an abnormally late age to begin drinking, but for whatever reason I simply hadn't gotten around to it before. Vodka, orange juice, and Mario Kart DUI constituted my alcoholic initiation. Oh, and also I learned never to sit on the toilet you're trying to puke into. It was a good night.

I met Biloxi Bob in November. His true name I never learned, and I've never seen him since; but I've always wondered if we might not cross paths again someday. Bob ran a cult in Biloxi: about half a dozen teenaged boys, runaways maybe, out of a wretched old house. They worked and gave him their money, and he stuffed them with trash about being the chosen ones (whatever that meant). When I heard about it from some locals, I went straight there. Not *real* smart, but I seriously believed I was invulnerable at this point. Indeed, it was well for me that I'd lately learned from the Orthodox how easily demons can pass for angels to the unwary, otherwise I might very well have been swayed by old Bob. As it was, I was tempted.

Not that I saw anything supernatural there, mind you. As a matter of fact, I've never seen anything that I couldn't explain as belonging to the natural order (not yet, anyhow). But the chosen one thing resonated for me. I *wanted* to be the chosen one. I've since come to perceive that obviously everybody is the chosen one, marked for some destiny within the Mystical Body of Christ that no one else can fulfill. "Are all apostles? Are all prophets? Are all teachers? Do all work miracles?" (1 Corinthians 12:29). But Bob and I talked for hours while his lost boys sat by; and, as much as a part of me wanted to believe, I finally concluded that this guy was neither a prophet nor a devil. Just a deluded old man with fake teeth. What had I hoped to accomplish by going there? To liberate his followers by eloquence, or maybe even force?—that old idea of mine about fighting perdition with karate? I suppose. It sounds silly now; but worse, it sounds selfish. Even if I had succeeded in so good a deed, it would have been for my own glory, not His. In the end, I simply walked out and never went back. Soon after, I returned to Montgomery to be arrested, as already told.

So. What in all of Creation was I looking for out there? God's truth—I really don't know. Sometimes I craved adventure—which, as I now see, I actually had in plenty—but to me it didn't count unless it involved fighting samurai or jumping out of exploding buildings. Sometimes I yearned for wisdom—inherently a laudable pursuit, but my motive and means were all wrong, and anyway real wisdom requires humility. I definitely hadn't yet progressed as far as having a hunger and thirst for holiness; I don't think that even occurred to me until I met Annabelle in '04, and it was another two years before I started trying to do anything about it. I guess, all said and done, I was looking for something to *devote* myself to: a mission or crusade of some kind, a Quest. But the very restlessness that sent me scampering across the continental states in my search also kept me from staying still long enough to find anything.

When I became a part of the Kai, that changed. I stayed in Jotun from early 2000 until mid-2003, absolutely *breathing* the martial arts, and up till then I had instinctively measured out my term of residency in any given place in terms of weeks. By '03, I was finally thinking in months—although enough bizarre and shattering things happened in the meantime that Jotun seemed to become a totally new place at least a few times during my stay.

There's an old adage to the effect that the best reason for studying warcraft is to become so expert that you'll never have to use it. On a small scale, I've witnessed that principle in action myself: would-be troublemakers at our parties tended to back down from our students simply because of the extreme confidence with which they carried themselves, thus averting outright violence. I suppose the worst reason is to become a more effective bully, and I fear we may have strayed into that particular usage a time or two as well. But the fact is, Josh and

T. and I didn't have any explicit reason for studying the arts. We just did it because we loved it.

Also, I think, we all felt the need for some kind of purpose in our lives and we hadn't yet glimpsed it anywhere else. Josh had been baptized Catholic, but his parents didn't practice the Faith or raise him in it; and JSC's an aggressively secular school. So he was firmly agnostic—though, thank God, the grace of Baptism still glimmered in him, awaiting its time to burst into flame. Sensei and T. were Christians as well, and I still considered myself Catholic; but none of us went to church, except perhaps on the high holy days, or thought much about acting out our beliefs in normal life. We had all managed to wrap our heads around the concept of the martial way: that the arts are not something one does but something one *lives*. ("The master shows his art in every movement.") And because all things work to the good for those who love God, He used that small understanding to awaken us to a far, far greater one.

Eventually.

The Best Move
in Chess

The next time you walk barefoot over hot pavement or sharp gravel, watch what happens to your hands. Automatically—without the consent of your will—they'll come up and start pressing downward trying to take some of the weight off your feet. It's a simple stimulus-response, as universal as the human nervous system, and we're all coded with similar responses to various types of pain or pressure. One of the most useful (to the person exploiting it, not the one experiencing it) is called cross-extendory reflex. It makes it all but impossible for me to use my free hand against an opponent who's locked my other hand in a certain way, and it's the basis of a lot of the wrist locks the cops like to use. In KJJ we have a whole chain of these locks all strung together—and because each of them keys off a neurologically patterned response in the lamentable recipient, executing all of them in sequence forces him to drop at the knees, come up on his toes, bend backward and then forward at the waist, run around in a circle, and finally hurl himself face-first to the earth (where, if he's adept enough, he can front-roll to his feet unharmed). We call it the Dance of Pain. As with anything, it can't work on 100% of all *Homo sapiens*—even bullets won't stop an attacker sufficiently drugged or enraged—but I've personally seen it used on a large number of people and have yet to see it fail. And almost every day of the week when we got together to train, Sensei would greet me and Josh not with a hug or a handshake but with this little dance of ours.

Aristotle says we become what we do. When we began, we were nowhere near as maniacally tough as we aspired to be; but Sensei treated us as if we already were, and thus were we forged. However!—there's a critical distinction to be observed between the inculcation of mental and physical toughness, and the transmission of actual techniques. The tenet we heard constantly in those early days (and went on to use constantly when we became teachers in turn) was, "Go slow and you'll go far." Naturally, we wanted to throw fireballs and flying death kicks from day one, but what we got was the most elemental basics, over and over and over and over, until Sensei was convinced we knew them well enough to start building on them. We didn't even get the second *half* of the first kata during those early weeks. I hear that in a good judo school you don't start learning throws for anything up to a few months: you just get thrown by everyone else in class. Thereby not only does the student learn to fall correctly, but the teacher gets to weed out the faint of heart. As Josh and I worked our way through the ranks over the next two and a half years, we saw quite a few people come in gung-ho and drift away fast when they realized you can't actually become a ninja master after one training montage. Some of them simply decided it wasn't for them, and told us so, and everyone was happy; but others kept promising to show up to class and ducking out every week, while at the same time bragging to visitors at our parties that they were "in the Kai." That was part of what had discouraged Sensei in the first place; but by the time we had grown enough to have a dojo and a weekly class again, the four of us were sufficiently solid that we could laugh off the posers. For now, it was just us and the dirt, pretty near every single day.

And 2000 seemed to be a blessed year in Jotun. Spring came fast and warm, and the rains all but scheduled themselves to accommodate our training sessions. For there was more than kata to be learned, my friends. KJJ's always been a grappling art, and we had a whole *universe* of butt-kickings ahead of us. Every class ended with a passel of matches, and we came to love aspirin and zheng-gu-shui (a Chinese ointment similar to Icy-Hot but stronger), "the grappler's best friends." T. and I once had a match in which I got so tangled that for a few seconds I literally couldn't figure out which direction was up. But jujitsu's my strong point, and I could generally beat him and

Josh with consistency; so Sensei and I became each other's nemeses in the squared circle, and Josh and T. developed a rivalry equaled only by Beowulf and Grendel. When the Kai was young, Josh wore a ponytail—it's hard to remember now that he's balder than Kojak—and our grandparents had been pestering him for years to get a respectable haircut. After a month or two of T. kneeling on his excess hair during their matches, we happened to go visit Grammy and Grampy one weekend and he casually expressed a wish to have it shortened, and I'll be thunderstruck if I've ever seen them mobilize so quickly. Couldn't have been fifteen minutes later Gramps had brought us to the nearest barber, insisting on paying for everything, terrified lest Josh should change his mind. And then Josh and T. became the stuff of our legends as time went by, having matches that went up to a whole hour of grueling agony at a time.

And they loved it—loved each other—spending half the time groaning or snarling, and the other half bantering and laughing. Once (and only Renee and I witnessed this, but I'll readily take my Bible oath on it) the two of them were grappling outside at day's end, and they started to steam, and a fog soon fell over the whole field—but the fog began with *them*.

And it gets more portentous yet. No doubt you recall my deliberately melodramatic promise to reveal our hidden trump card; well, it was revealed to me and Josh under conditions even more melodramatic, except they were brought about by God Himself—and somehow, He gets away with stuff that no novelist would ever dare to try. T. graduated from high school in late May, and the three of us—me, Josh, and Sensei—were naturally in attendance. It was an outdoor ceremony in mid-afternoon and, well, let's see—how do I put this. . . Okay, we got bored. Somewhere in the third unnecessary speech by someone nobody had heard of, the three of us snuck away to a nearby hilltop and Sensei chose that moment to unveil the third portion of KJJ's martial trinity: *escrima*.

Escrima comes from the Philippines, and it's hard-core well past the point of clinical insanity. The Filipinos developed it during the Spanish occupation in the 1800s, and they were known for simply charging into the swords and guns of their oppressors and killing them by the dozen before succumbing to their wounds. Apparently our military started carrying the .45 caliber pistol solely because we needed something powerful enough to knock them down in mid-charge. It's a very simple art, based on the machete techniques they'd learned in a lifetime of clearing the jungle, and its underlying assumption is that you don't care how horribly you die as long as you can drag a few enemies down to Hell with you when you go. The art is also known as Arnis and Kombaton, and a great many contemporary schools claim to have its secrets. But Master Montalban actually studied in the Philippines in the '70s, and had taken Sensei and his classmates to help teach a seminar to the American Special Forces in Kentucky a few years before—so, through whatever quirk of Providence, Josh and I got the real stuff suddenly hurled at us that fateful afternoon. 'Course, Sensei wasn't dumb enough to give us live blades on our very first day, so we started out learning the twelve basic strikes with the hard rattan sticks he kept in his trunk. And as we stood on that hilltop in the shining golden sunlight, a shadow crossed us and a black lightning-front came rolling in from nowhere. I remember thinking at the time, *I can never write about this. No one would ever believe it.* Well, that was over a decade ago, and I'm writing it now. I trust you to trust me, and to perceive that life offers moments which surpass any fiction or poetry. Thus, in the thunder and rain, we were baptized as escrimadors.

I mentioned earlier that every art has its weakness. Ours is also our strength: we strive to master several different styles and combat ranges in order to adapt more efficiently to many potential scenarios. If we find ourselves facing a striker, we grapple, and vice versa—if he's both, we find something stick-like to hit him with. The downside is that we're not exhaustively trained in any one combat range. If I found myself facing a really expert grappler in a small room where I couldn't avoid grappling, I'd be in serious trouble. ("Bite his jugular," is actually our only half-jesting rule-of-thumb for this situation.) Now, a great many people like to say that size doesn't matter in a fight. Why not say speed and skill don't matter while you're about it? Obviously everything matters in a fight, by no means excluding *luck*. Other things being equal, the bigger guy will win four falls out of five—which is why it behooves me to make sure other things aren't equal. Boxing rightly has weight divisions because if your only option is your fists and the other guy is a hundred pounds heavier than you, it probably won't be much of a fight; but a rapist or a mugger is unlikely to be so scrupulous in choosing only victims of his own size. Hence, we train to provide ourselves and our students with multiple different options.

It's also worth pointing out that size and strength aren't necessarily commensurate. I knew a rugby player called John back in Jotun who was smaller than me, but he could bench-press two hundred and fifty pounds. (Ah, the ruggers. More on them later.) But strength is of limited use unless you understand leverage. Some things you can figure out for yourself, through experience or logic—but in studying a martial art, you draw upon the things figured out by the logic and experience of thousands of warriors throughout time. Believe me, they've thought of things you haven't. Chesterton defines a Catholic as someone who has plucked up the courage to face the inconceivable fact that something else is wiser than he is. So too in the martial arts. But this is precisely where the parallel to Christianity becomes intensely interesting, and you must pardon me if I wax philosophical for a moment.

You see, our old friend Lane was unfortunately one of those who drifted in and out of the Kai a number of times, and I ultimately lost track of him for a few years after 2003. But apart from our wrastlin' rivalry, he and I also had (indeed, have) a long-standing theological dispute as well, and we actually picked it right back up when I ran into him in a bar in Burlington in '09. Not to put too fine a point on it, Lane was espousing subjectivism: if you believe a thing, then—for *you*—it is the truth. Ergo, no debate need exist between, say, a Quaker and a Buddhist, or a Moslem and a Manichee. In actuality—although it never stopped us—operating from this premise makes all argument impossible right at the outset; and in any case, the verities of the Creed are not susceptible to laboratory demonstration. What I could do, however, was to demonstrate that objective truth exists in a different arena, one that we both respected. Because whether anyone in the world acknowledges the fact or not, there *is* a right and a wrong way to throw a punch.

Here again the importance of an empty tea-cup manifested itself. Josh, having no martial background at all, simply did what he was told and soon became our best kenpo guy. People who came to us with "I took a year of tae kwon this or that" or "I'm a yellow belt in something or other bo" invariably thought they knew how to punch and had to be broken of bad habits. I was no different. When Sensei caught me throwing punches with my arms fully extended, he almost smacked me. "You'll hyper-extend your elbow that way. You might as well put your thumb inside your fist. Always keep a bow in your arm." But the hardest part was getting people to use their hips. Any boxer knows a good punch comes from the legs, not the arms—after all, punching is what they do—yet somehow in the Oriental styles you constantly see reverse punches being thrown from a stance that's frozen from the waist down.

Where I really gave Sensei grief, however, was in the grappling phase. I was good enough by this time that I could beat almost anyone who rolled with us, and I even beat him once in the first couple of months (though largely by luck, as his gi got twisted up in my feet), so it was hard for me to accept that I was doing things wrong. But when I could believe and obey, I began to pick up all sorts of knowledge: not major new moves, but ways of tweaking and improving what I already knew. The crucial skill I learned in this time was how to take a proper reverse mount (the position from which you choke someone out, my favorite of all techniques): not by wrapping your legs around your enemy's torso from behind, but by sinking your heels into his femorals and pulling his legs apart so he can't maneuver. We call it "putting your hooks in." The best cinematic execution of this move I have yet seen, oddly enough, was not in a kung-fu flick but in the opening minutes of *The Two Towers* when Gollum starts choking Sam. I love Samwise Gamgee—so much so that I half-expect to meet him when, God willing, I make it to Heaven—but a bunch of us went and saw this movie in the theater, and when the hooks sank into Sammy's femorals, we were suddenly all cheering for Gollum (somewhat to the consternation of our fellow movie-goers).

Meanwhile, T. was becoming our premier escrimador.

We have a stick pattern called six-count drill in which you and a partner attack the crap out of each other in a pre-set sequence of strikes and blocks (three of each, in alternation, hence the name), to develop speed and coordination, and also to accustom you to having a stick swung at you at top velocity so you don't panic if it ever happens for real. First time Josh and I saw it, Sensei and T. were drilling so hard and so fast that after a minute or so we could *smell* it too: the impact friction creates a strong, acrid odor, as of scorching wood. We thought this was the awesomest thing in the history of anything ever, and spent years trying to drill hard enough to produce actual smoke. Before long, we too could create the burning smell, but to my knowledge no one in the Kai ever succeeded in bringing forth smoke or sparks. When we were first learning the pattern, we once lost sight of the "go slow, go far" admonition, and Josh cracked me on the finger hard enough that, to this day, I've got a barely noticeable calcium deposit on my knuckle. Of course, when we were at our black belt camp two years later, I acciden-tally hit him in the hand with a machete (a dull one, thankfully), so I guess it all balanced. Yep: good times.

Such was our good fortune, to stumble into an art which strives to be (if I may take St. Paul a trifle out of context) "all things to all men." It's said that while a good warrior uses his strengths, a great one uses his weaknesses; the point of KJJ is to facilitate this. Being big and slow, for example, can be an advantage once you and your adversary are rolling around on the floor. If you find yourself outmatched in one martial aspect, you have others to fall back on—strikes, or throws, or ground-work, or (failing all else) an improvised weapon of one kind or another. Which aspect is superior? Well—what is the best move in chess? It all depends on what pieces are on the board.

Such too was Heaven's mercy to me, that I found a simple cause to devote myself to in a place full of people I loved. In Jotun, I learned to become a part of something larger than myself, and to finish something I had started. In Jotun, I took the first few steps on the road to regaining my honor. And now— now I can no longer put off telling you how I came to lose it in the first place.

failures

My father's Christian name is James—like his father, and his father before him. The reason I don't have a "IV" after my name is that our middle names are all different. (Mine's Blaise, after the patron of throats: anti-vampire saint par excellence.) Story goes, my great-grandfather went by Jim and Grampa Toner went by James; Dad was Jimmy, and I'm Jamey. Why he waited for a third son to pass on the name, he's never really said—and what permutation of "James" now remains for my own potential progeny is also unclear. Some of my friends have suggested "Jameson," but even I hesitate to accept the risk of confusing my whiskey with my child.

Now, the Toner men are college men—and military men. When I finished high school in '95, I had no solid notion of what I wanted to do with myself, so I sort of vaguely went to college and sort of vaguely majored in English. And something awfully strange happened to me there. Over the long years since then, I've done more than enough mean and stupid things to make this book a confession rather than a memoir; but even from my current vantage, midway through my three-score years and ten, I still believe *this* thing was out of my control.

Basically it was what Lewis calls *sehnsucht*: an over-whelming, fathomless yearning for we know not what, an inconsolable longing with no definable object. Everyone feels it. Sunsets and symphonies and Frodo sailing away into the West all stir it up in us. It's that feeling of, "God, I wish. . ." and the inevitable trailing off because, what are we wishing for? Something, something the soul is born already missing, already homesick to find again although we've never found it, never seen it, barely glimpsed its glowing, fading shadow on the earth. I hadn't been at 'Bama for a week when it set in— mildly enough at first, as mere restlessness, but rapidly esca-lating until it drove me out to roam the streets at night. I didn't drink or do drugs, I didn't get in fights or cause trouble, I didn't chase women (in fact I didn't date until I was twenty-two); I just prowled the town, fulminating, like a crazy person. Night after night after night.

You may well ask what became of my studies. My teachers and parents raised the same question. There was, I'm fairly certain, nothing mentally wrong with me; but I was half-frenzied with a spiritual pressure, as if my inmost self were struggling to hatch or pupate. I can't even remember what classes I took that semester. French, I think. And I must've taken English, I was majoring in English. I also took a little tae kwon do and hapkido, but I couldn't focus even on them. I did have one minor adventure during this period: I was walking through downtown sometime after midnight when a completely random psychopath abruptly started chasing me *with his car*, screaming out the window for my death, for no perceptible reason whatsoever. Thank God I can climb like a spider monkey; I went over a ten-foot chain-link in about two seconds, dropped into the lot beyond, and was instantly blinded and deafened by flashing lights and blaring sirens. Turns out I'd vaulted into the local Chrysler dealership. The alarms frightened away my new friend, and I re-climbed the fence and ran for cover. Made for a more exciting night than usual—but it made no difference to the *sehnsucht*, good or bad.

In short, I didn't do very well at the U of A. When I came home in December, I spent Christmas break trying to decide what else to do with myself, since clearly I wasn't meant to be in college at this particular juncture in my career. With little virtue and no wisdom to guide me, and with my obstinacy in refusing advice, I fell abysmally under the glamour of a single idea: proving myself. Precisely what I was to prove, and to whom, remained hazy; but I knew it somehow involved feats of arms and "adventures" (which at this point still meant to me the sort of thing you see in action movies). There's a passage in Jorge Luis Borges in which he describes reaching a certain age and having his father hand him a dagger and say, "Go let someone know you're a man." Didn't matter how or why— all that mattered was not coming home until he had picked a knife fight and walked away victorious. I remember reading it, years later, and nodding in perfect recognition. That urge, that need, to "prove something"—so universal, so compelling, and so profoundly, astronomically *stupid*. For God's sake, can't a man prove himself by volunteering at a soup kitchen?

But that never occurred to me. Instead, I joined the Army. An admirable choice in the abstract, even if it was made for silly reasons; and I like to think that if I could quantum leap my present self back into that fumbling Toner past, I'd make a halfway decent infantryman. (I suppose we all feel that way about some bygone time in our lives.) Back then, though, I just didn't have it together. Physically, I was perfectly fine—I could run and shoot and do push-ups as well as the next fellow—but somehow I couldn't seem to do anything else right. Ever see *Full Metal Jacket*? If so, you already see where I'm going with this, and yes: I was Private Pyle. To this day, I can't properly make a hospital corner on a bed. I got the snot tear-gassed out of me (pardon the colloquialism, but it's the exact and literal truth) because I couldn't figure out my gas mask. Map-reading, mine-disarming, even sock-rolling, for pity's sake—I'd never been forced to be organized before, and I was *far* less grown-up than I should have been at that age. Indeed, it's been a recurrent motif in my life that wherever I find myself, I turn out to be a few years behind where I ought to be. But still, I could've tried harder; they called me "unmotivated," and they were right. After a certain point, I was barely holding on, waiting for Basic Training to be over, rather than rising up to master it.

I spent February and March of '96 at Fort Benning, Georgia, being the very worst soldier in Bravo Company. Then I failed to clear my rifle on the firing range. After we'd filed out and were pulling triggers at the sky to be sure our chambers were empty, mine went off. They were only blanks—thank God—and they were aimed off toward nothing at all—thank God—but it remains, I think, my most disgraceful moment. Not a good memory, and you'll pardon my not wishing to dwell on it. After that, they sent me home.

And I joined the Navy. Yes, this is true. Because I hadn't finished Basic, I got some kind of conditional discharge, and the military decided to give me another chance. Again, I believe my intentions were good—the desire to redeem my name and continue trying to make something of myself—but I did only a little better the second time around. At least I finished boot camp, in August of '96 at Great Lakes, Illinois. Then I went off to Pensacola, Florida, for training in my MOS (military occupational specialty), which was code-breaking.

And *that* was actually pretty cool. I got a Top Secret clearance, and I got to go into sealed chambers and learn about esoteric machinery which I guess I shouldn't describe. I must admit I looked at myself in the mirror once or twice and Sean

Conneried, "Blaise. James Blaise."

Pensa-cola was nice, too. We lived in suites of four rooms, three men to a room, and I got to be pretty good buddies with my suite-mates, all of whom (naturally enough, being eighteen- and nineteen-year-old servicemen) shared my love of rough-housing and watching *Hercules* and *Xena*. Matter of fact, the boys elected me suite leader after a couple of weeks—I honestly don't know exactly why. I suppose I got on well enough with most of them, and I was also the wrestling champ of our little circle. In any case, the position had no real authority or responsibility to speak of, besides telling people to clear their pizza boxes out of the common room, but the military is the military and *somebody* has to be in charge.

Alas. I was smart enough to get picked for cryptology based on my aptitude scores; but when it came down to it, the actual schooling was all math, and I'm abominable at math. I ended up failing out of the program, so they put me in a holding company while they figured out what to do with me instead. They also had me talk to a lieutenant whose name I've forgotten, who tried to counsel me; he suggested I consider being a religious petty officer, that is a chaplain's assistant, which now I sort of wish I'd done. But—by way of illustrating my maturity level at the time—I remember him talking about freedom and self-discipline and how an adult, unlike a child, can go and eat a dozen candy bars for lunch but knows better than to do so; and my first thought was, "Ooh, I *could* go eat a dozen candy bars, couldn't I?" That would be funnier if only it weren't true.

So, I returned to my rambling ways, pacing the perimeter of Corry Field all night and brooding on my "destiny," which I felt sure must be something grand. (Remember my desire to be "the chosen one"?) I still felt called beyond all horizons, and thought that somehow that call must free me from the oaths and obligations I had freely taken upon myself. And in those hubris-addled ramblings, I missed daily muster one morning and got sent to the restricted barracks. I've sometimes thought there is perhaps no failure committable through foolishness or sloth that I haven't committed. In the restricted barracks, I tried to "step up" to a petty officer and got knocked on my ass—and that was likewise the end of my brief, abortive maritime tenure. Never saw a ship. I was brigged at the Naval Air Station for a week or so, sent back to the restricted barracks, and eventually out-processed with an Other Than Honorable discharge. There are five kinds—honorable, general, OTH, bad conduct discharge (or "big chicken dinner"), and dishonorable, which I believe is reserved for murder and desertion and suchlike. Mine? Mine was bad enough.

It was April of '97 when I got back home, and my father and I had much to say to one another, none of it good. For whatever it's worth now, I need to say that I was wrong about everything. For whatever it's worth—I'm sorry I let you down, Dad.

TWO

The Golden Age

PART 2

A Growing Family

So. Three years after falling into the uttermost depths as soon as I came out of the starting gate, I was more or less back on my feet in Jotun and treading a less familiar track to self-realization. And once I consented to be an organ in a greater body—once I became a part of something—I began to see that I'd been trying to define myself in a vacuum. There is really no working way to describe a person except by the way in which he or she relates to other people. Even the Lord God is a Holy Family.

Luckily, it so happened that my group of friends was swiftly expanding. Our housemate Rob had a friend called Lissa who was moving out of the dorms and looking for a place to stay in town, and we had no objection to splitting the rent six ways instead of five, so she moved into the House and became exposed to the martial mania then rampant. Sensei's high school buddies Arnold and D.J. joined us. T.'s friend Renee came on board. And of course, half a dozen other people drifted in and out as the weeks went by. Josh was all done at JSC and working at a restaurant, and I was working at a (now-defunct) gas station just outside of town; both of us put in only as many hours as we needed to earn rent, food, and beer money, and the rest of our time went to training.

Well—okay, that's not *technically* true. *Technically*, the House somehow became a titanic focal point that summer for all the major parties in town. Not only every weekend, but most typically two or three times per weekend, dozens of people— both friends and total strangers—would cram the place to the rafters and rock to the vaults of Heaven. On the ground floor, where the Kai held sway, there was an unbreakable edict against country, rap, or techno; classic rock was welcome enough when we needed a change, but mostly we slammed out to the Irish stuff: Flogging Molly, Dropkick Murphys, and of course the sovereign Pogues. The substance of most parties was what we called "jigging," though none of us could actu- ally dance a jig—basically it meant linking arms and jumping around as loudly and destructively as possible. And—hoo, boy—we just drank like drowning fish. One of the mainstays was a drink invented by Lane, originally called the Black Malibu (same as a Black Russian except with Malibu rum instead of coffee liqueur) but later called the Blackout because—well, for obvious reasons. Among the core group, drunken kata out on the lawn became an amazingly fun tradition; and one way or another, Lissa and I developed our own little practice of drunkenly diagramming sentences on the House message board. It all went to excess, no doubt; but at least, as Josh recently remarked, we'll *never* have to look back on our twenties and say, "Gee, I wish we'd cut loose a little."

But now I fear I must record the manner in which we became a House divided. As I say, the first floor was our domain; there lay the kitchen, the living room, and one of the two bathrooms. On the second floor, a DMZ where no partier ventured except to pass through to the top floor, was the other bathroom and three bedrooms—one belonging to Rob, one shared by Lane and Lissa (platonically), and one shared by me and Josh. The third floor, AKA the loft, belonged to Topper. Lest that should sound inequitable, recall that Lissa and I were late additions to the living arrangements, and Topper had been at the House the longest. Anyway, there were no walls in the loft, so it couldn't function practically as a bedroom for more than one person. No one minded this. The genesis of the troubles arose in smoke like Mephistopheles—marijuana smoke. Vermont, as you may know, is something of a hot-bed of pot culture; and, as a small-town college, JSC was particularly overrun. My intense personal prejudice against pot dates from my time in Jotun, where I saw that stuff turn *way* too many once-bright people into the slinking specters of human beings. (Doubtless the same can be said of alcohol; I didn't say it was a rational prejudice.) At all events, we had forbidden the use of any controlled substances within the small sphere of our hegemony—but when Topper declared the loft a weed-welcome sin-den, the parties quickly polarized into the drinking crowd and the drug crowd.

And ah, one night, one certain night, two ladies came to call, both freshmen, strangers to the House and our peculiar ways. One went up the steps, into the pall and out of this tale forever. The other stayed below. Her name was Gwen: a singer, and a fellow Catholic. Somehow we had an instant ineluctable connection, and ended up sharing a rocking chair and pouring out our hearts to one another as if we'd been friends for years. I remember tipsily trying to explain my writing/fighting dichotomy—that I wield a pen with my left hand but a stick with my right, and what shape they make when you hold them perpendicular. And she took my left and said, "This is the hand that's going to make your dreams come true."

Thus, in the gloaming of my adolescence, I stumbled into my first romantic relationship. She was good to me. I've only had a very few girlfriends, and they've all concurred upon the fact that I'm a difficult person to date—which I can readily believe. (*I* certainly wouldn't date me; in fact, I'd unquestionably kick the ever-loving bollocks out of myself if I had to spend half an hour with myself.) But Gwen accepted my—or rather, *our*, since Josh and I were kind of a package deal—martial obsession with patience, and taught me the rudiments of gentleness. Think Eva Marie Saint in *On the Waterfront*.

It also turned out, not too surprisingly in a town only big enough for two degrees of separation, that she was an acquaintance of Josh's younger sister: my other cousin, Sarah, who hasn't yet appeared in this book simply because she hadn't yet appeared in the Kai. She was (I believe) a sophomore at this time—that is, just finishing her sophomore year and about to become a junior. We'd traveled in largely disparate social circles during the semester, but by some chance or design, she ended up spending a great deal of time with us that summer. For one thing, my first nephew—Benjamin, emerging scion of the new generation of Toners—was born in Ohio, and Josh, Sarah, and I took a road trip in old Seamus, Josh's grizzled Impala, to attend the baptism. We also sort of swung through Hampton Beach and Niagara Falls, by way of celebrating Josh's graduation. And when we got back, she and Gwen grew to be closer than heretofore, which brought Sarah to the House ever more frequently. Before long, our enthusiasm had rubbed off on my fairer cousin (sorry, Josh), and she too became a part of our little legion.

That September, early in my twenty-third year, Sensei finally decided it was time. He, Josh, T. and I packed our sticks, belts, and uniforms, gathered our resolve, and headed for Connecticut to present ourselves to Master Montalban. T. had visited the main dojo before, but Sensei had so far endeavored to shield me and Josh from his own sensei, for reasons we would soon perceive and rue. Our teacher's teacher was hosting a kenpo seminar that weekend, with several prominent schools—one from as far away as Frisco—coming together to share their secrets. And don't get me wrong: the seminar was *awesome*. We got to learn some highly advanced stuff and meet some top-notch martial artists; and there's nothing like a few days of non-stop training, punctuated by brief periods of sleep on hard wrestling mats, to make one feel tough (a few days later, when the feeling returns to one's legs). Also, I learned a qi-based resuscitation technique called the kiatsu there. I've since used it twice, on people choked out during matches—one by a guy called Jared and one by myself—and it almost instantly restored awareness to people who would ordinarily have spent the next few minutes "jelly-fishing" and awoken totally disoriented. (This, incidentally, is why you tap out when the other guy has you in a choke. It's not worth it.) Before I speak of Master Montalban, I'd like to say a word on the topic of qi.

The name embodies a complex and only fragmentarily translatable concept; it's variously conveyed as "life," "breath," "blood," "spirit," and—my personal favorite—"energy." The Japanese render it *ki* and the Chinese *chi*; I spell it with a Q in order to allow either pronunciation. In essence it refers to the mysterious, but not *necessarily* mystical, force which binds together the body and the soul. I must say plainly that it's not a debatable phenomenon, but as objectively real as, say, germs or electromagnetism or any other unseen engine of the visible world. My "battle buddy" Stull, at Fort Benning, could focus it so strongly that when he held his hands out, you could feel the air tingle. But as I say, it's all theoretically explicable if you don't care to believe in the unseen. The Chinese mapped out the qi currents of the body through acupuncture millennia ago, and the modern findings of Western science regarding the electrical paths of the nervous system agree uncannily with that ancient mysticism. Nor should this be surprising to a Christian. Since Christ is Truth, we ought to have the humility to learn from the glimpses of verity that He bequeathed to the heathen mind. Even our great feast of Christmas, after all, is originally an assimilated pagan solstice tradition; and half the theology of St. Thomas Aquinas is based upon the teachings of Aristotle, the pagan sage whom he is said to have "baptized." Indeed, it was St. Thomas who taught us that since there is but one Truth, science and faith can never genuinely conflict (although they may seem to)—and therefore, whether you choose to understand qi rationally or preternaturally, it is nevertheless the prerogative of the Church to baptize and assimilate its truths.

Now, Master Montalban was known as a gifted weaver of qi. I saw it myself, a little. He was known as a powerful martial artist, and we saw the reflection of that every day in our own master, his student. And he was known as an innovator and organizer, which was clear enough in the fact that other masters from around the nation were congregating at his school. All that being the case, I can only think he must once have been—at least potentially—a very great warrior. Because when Josh and I encountered him, he was already sliding into decay. Like the Romans before the Visigoths, he still retained the shadow of greatness; but there was definitely something the matter with the man. For one thing, he kept badgering us—all of us—for money, and more money. New fees kept manifesting themselves, and the subject cropped up out of nowhere again and again. Of course, even the wisest man can have financial troubles, I reasoned; only he seemed so waspish, so querulous, in his demands. And even odder, he couldn't seem to stop talking once he started—on any subject. Not wishing to hyperbolize, I once kept an eye on a dashboard clock while he spoke disjointedly for forty minutes straight about the lineage of our art: an interesting topic to be sure, except that we were climbing into Sensei's already running car at the time, and Sensei was literally standing through the whole monologue with one leg inside the door and one out. I sincerely wondered if he might have some species of Tourette's that disconnected whatever brain circuit tells one to stop talking.

Nope. Drugs. Sensei didn't tell us then; it was his teacher, after all. But a few months later, he and Josh accompanied Master Montalban and a few of his other black belts on a martial tour of the west coast (I didn't have the money for the trip, and I can't honestly say I regret missing it, based on Josh's report). It's not my intention in this account to linger on anyone's faults—even my own—so, briefly: in spending a week with the man, Josh got to witness uncontrolled rage, adultery, and a fair amount of drug use. Worst of all, to my mind, he reportedly gave the drugs to his senior students to carry onto the plane for him. This was pre-9/11 and security was looser, but—still. It's too much to overlook in even the best of teachers. We visited his dojo a couple more times that autumn. Lissa got to meet him. Sensei received his *ni-dan*, his second-degree black belt. And then, as the ice settled over the roads and our desire to see Connecticut steadily dwindled, a time came when we simply stopped going back.

But as grim as those moments were (and worst of all for Sensei), the closing months of the year were happy ones. We trained, we partied, we worked a bit—we enjoyed each other, and life. One frosty night, for instance, Josh and T. and I were cruising the back roads with our Kai brother D.J., talking nonsense, when we crested a hill and saw a neighboring town lit up far below and the kindled galaxies far above; and Josh said, "Pull over. This calls for kata." So we got out and stood in the starlight with a fenced-off cow pasture at our backs, and ran through the first three forms together; then D.J., who hadn't yet learned the fourth kata—better known as "Vortex," Form Four—stood back to observe. Josh and T. and I were just beginning when he said, "Uh, guys—" and we shushed him. "Guys," he said again, and we snapped at him to keep his yap shut during kata. "Guys, there's a bull coming," he insisted. At this point I turned and shouted, "D.J., there's a fence between us and the—" Then I stopped, because there was a six-foot gap in the fence *right behind us* and there was indeed a bull coming— not quite charging yet, but clearly picking up speed. So we all shrieked like kindergarteners, sprinted back to the car, and peeled out as if every devil in Hell was on our tail. To this day, Josh and I still refer to that kata as "Run Away From The Cow," Form Four.

Meanwhile, the Kai kept growing. And as imperfect as its members inevitably were, the thing itself was becoming greater than its parts—a choir of swords in which every soul illuminated unknown facets of all the others. I do seriously believe that during those few short years, the Kai was a vessel of secret grace for quite a few people in Jotun, and we were all blessed to toil and sweat and bleed together. It was fortunate, moreover, that we grew and bonded so quickly in our earliest days—because our first great trial was already on the horizon.

七

After This Our Exile

We were still kids in a lot of ways. Our corporate theme song was "We Are the Knuckleheads" by the Bloodhound Gang. Our preferred method of greeting was to grab each other's butts. And our greatest inspiration in moments of frustration or fatigue was an anime (that's a Japanese cartoon, in case you're my dad) called *Dragonball Z*. Even now I'll aver that one could do a good deal worse in the inspiration department. The show's basic template was this: the good guys are warriors who keep encountering evil warriors far stronger than they are. In each new encounter, they get the stuffing beaten out of them; then they go away and train maniacally for multiple episodes, come back, and beat the stuffing out of the bad guys. Then even stronger bad guys come along and the template repeats. It's not Shakespeare or anything. But man, if you need a mental image to fortify your willpower for one last push-up or stick drill, it's hard to beat the heroes of DBZ on a windswept mountaintop, howling at the top of their lungs and radiating golden light as they lift themselves in the air with nothing but their qi. Throw in some "Eye of the Tiger" and you've got yourself an extra spurt of adrenaline right there.

In short, all our youthful energies were dedicated to the arts, our honor and joy, but we weren't thinking ahead beyond the next training session or maybe the next party. Anyone could've told us we wouldn't be able to practice outside in Vermont forever; but we were woefully unprepared for the coming of the snows. Once again, Josh came through for the Kai as 2001 crept onto the calendars, making calls and following leads until he found us a dojo. (Sensei's old place in Stowe was just a back room in a local store, and they ended up using it for something else when his class drifted away in tag-end '99.) Our new battleground was a ski lodge in the looming peaks that frowned over Jotun town. By the time we got there, though, things in our group had already begun to change. *Everything* would change in time—everything but the arts.

For one thing, Gwen and I broke up in December. She was looking for a more mature, long-term sort of relationship than I wasn't even remotely capable of, and we found ourselves quarreling whenever we saw each other. But, while it was a sad separation—always is, I guess—it wasn't bitter, and we're actually still friends today. Josh, for his part, was still single after breaking up with Mindy in March; his dating hiatus ultimately lasted nearly two years. On the other hand, Sensei and T. were both newly involved—with Lissa and Renee, respectively. Now: if you question whether this was such a good idea, you might have a case in the abstract. We were all part of an extremely tight-knit group, and "office romances" can always lead to complications (especially when the office's domestic product is radical physical violence). In practice, though, I'm not convinced that our intra-Kai dating brought about any more drama than, well, any and all dating at that age might have done; and anyhow the thing was inevitable. You can't throw red-blooded college-aged men and women into such intense proximity and not expect to see some sparks, and a level of mutual trust and understanding existed among us for which we sought in vain in the world outside. (Remember again that JSC was a highly secular environment and little there could be relied upon.) Josh, our brother Arnold, and I all wound up loving ladies of the Kai. It was simply the way of things.

But that was down the road a bit. Early in '01, it was all swingin' sticks and chokin' fools, and our ranks kept growing. Sarah's friend Mariko joined us, and picked up a complex two-stick attack sequence so quickly that Josh and I (for whom it had taken weeks to master) almost throttled her. Josh's old college buddy Merrin joined us, and—being particularly interested in grappling—became sort of my first unofficial protégé. T.'s friend Ned joined us and was, honestly, best known for being the goofy kid in the group. But he was *our* goofy kid, and he knew we had his back (indeed, he had a tendency to get maudlin about it when he'd had a few). Alas, whatever he used for deodorant was legendarily non-functional, and he tended to wear a wife-beater to class. I remember walking around the room once, supervising pairs of partners who were studying a grappling technique executed from side mount—that is, a position in which the bottom fighter is on his back and the top fighter is perpendicular and belly-to-belly, pinning him down. Arnold, my poor beloved comrade, had been matched with Ned, and as I passed by, he was on the bottom and his whole face was hidden in his partner's armpit—all but his eyes, which met mine with a look of such misery and despair that all I could do was shriek with laughter and leave him to his fate.

The weekly class was not a solemn undertaking. As we grew, we unavoidably became more organized; soon everyone had belts, ranging from white through the many colors to black, and we all lined up by rank at the start of class with Sensei up front (generally flanked by T., Josh, and myself, as the senior students) and bowed in. The kenpo bow is forward at the waist, maintaining eye contact, while presenting the right fist covered by the left palm to symbolize the control of spirit over strength. That moment was quiet and serious; the next three hours were loud, ribald, and silly—while still being arduous and efficient. Usually we had calisthenics, spent the bulk of class doing drills, and then did kata for awhile. Class always ended with grappling matches, in which anyone might be thrown in with anyone

(Sensei was fond of pitting the smaller girls against Arnold, who has actually been mistaken for an M-1 tank on more than one occasion) while the rest of us called helpful suggestions or helpfully chanted, "Two men enter—one man leaves! Two men enter—one man leaves!" Sometimes Sensei would freeze the match and take the opportunity to teach the grapplers a new move they might use from whatever exotic position they had rolled themselves into. Anyone who won a bout with something they'd just learned that night got extra props.

During the week, I spent a lot of time working with Merrin. He was renting a small house, not far from *the* House, with my dear friend Cherie—the first person I'd grown close with when I came to Jotun back in '98. She was marvelously tolerant of our crashing around the living room struggling to disassemble one another's bodily machinery. Merrin practiced some manner of wiccanism, and occasionally went by the nickname "Merlin" (he was taken aback to learn that my middle name was Blaise, the wizard who taught Arthur's teacher); it was he who pointed out my affinity to the crow, calling it my "spirit animal." I'd started reading a little about my faith by this time, and I knew that St. Francis of Assisi had a special bond with his brother the wolf and his sisters, the birds of the wood (as a fellow vaga-bond, I had a great love of St. Francis already), so I concluded there was no peril of paganism in accepting the crow as my brother, a fellow child of God. I still greet them aloud wherever I see them.

So, the days went by; we went our own way, kept our own counsel, and put off going back to Connecticut. Somehow Master Montalban got wind of the fact that we had a dojo again, and a flourishing family—I suppose Sensei must've innocently mentioned it in an email or something. What our martial grandfather failed to understand was that no money was coming in from all these students. We were asked for a nominal monthly fee to help rent the space at the ski lodge; but we were all destitute, and most of us simply gave Sensei whatever we could. The balance of the costs, he made up out of his own pocket. If he had really shared his negative profits with our home dojo, it would have been tantamount to sending his sensei a bill every month.

This did not satisfy Master Montalban. I confess that I visualize the man brooding over desiccated flies in a vast iron web, tapping his many feet and awaiting his tribute; and I can't help pointing out that he had no conceivable legal or moral claim on any money his student might possibly have earned by opening a school of his own, any more than my father owes a percentage of his salary to the doctoral board that gave him his Ph.D. It wasn't a restaurant franchise. But I'm trying not to dwell on the master's faults here. Suffice it to say that as the days grew longer and the buds began to blossom, the subject must have been festering in his mind—and one night, after weeks of radio silence, Sensei got an email.

I got to read it. All the senior students did. For me and Josh, it merely confirmed all our very worst impressions: the thing wasn't written by a sage and warrior, but by a rotten child with a syntax picked up from watching South Park. Yeah, there was obscenity in it—even disparagements of our teacher's penis size—enough to make me *almost* pity the one who wrote it. But my sympathy was for Sensei, for whom this was no shadowy patriarch but his personal mentor for years—in a way, I think, a father figure of sorts, although he rarely speaks of his old master these days. I never saw Montalban again.

In this way, our great schism came about. Sensei, at twenty-three, suddenly stood alone, a *pater familias*, and we his students became his sole responsibility. At the start of the next class, he sat us all down and told us where we stood: we were now a rogue academy, a Kai in exile. As a *ni-dan*, Sensei could still bestow the rank of *sho-dan*, first-degree black belt—but as long as we were his students, we could never progress beyond that stage. He would continue teaching anyone who wanted to learn, he said; but certainly there would be no hard feelings if anyone wanted to seek out a teacher with his lineage intact.

I hope there's no suspense at this point in the narrative. None of us ever thought of our Kai as primarily a school: it was always a family foremost. Since that night, we've gone on to produce nine black belts and two junior *sho-dan* (students under the age of sixteen), and not one of us regrets that we can't sew this or that decorative patch onto our belts to indicate second or third degree. The skill, the discipline, the fellowship—that's what matters. In any case, most of the *kyu* ranks (the younger students) had never made the pilgrimage to Connecticut, and they acknowledged no sensei but Sensei.

Once that was settled, we had to ratchet things up a notch. The ski lodge closed with the advent of spring thaw, and our classes moved back to the soccer fields where Josh and I first began to learn kata. T. had earned his brown, the penultimate belt, under Montalban; now it was time to produce the first *sho-dan* of our own. For me and Josh, the next couple of months were all about supporting our brother—and, of course, pushing him to train like a dangerous psychopath. When May came, Mary's month, the time arrived at last for the great ordeal of which so many cryptic tales had told: black belt camp. Arnold's parents owned and ran a dairy farm in Mortonville, the next town over (AKA Mo-Vegas, City of Lights), and they kindly let us use their land for our three-day trial of the heart.

It started with a full-out three-hour class as the morning sky went from grey to gold. After that, we broke our fast with fruit, granola, and nightmarish quantities of water. (Would it be indelicate to say I'd never peed so much in my whole life as I did during that camp? Perhaps so. Let's forget I said that.) Then we inaugurated that hated phrase which is now an ancient and venerable tradition of the Kai: "Time to run the hill." Half a mile from the main road up the sharp ascent to the long steep driveway and so back to the dairy farm—it wasn't as bad as the hill I grew up on, but then again I didn't have to take that hill at the double-quick. After the run we had a couple of hours to work individually on drills or katas or whatever the *kyu* ranks felt they needed to improve upon. Here it was especially incumbent on T. to hone his talents as an instructor, with me and Josh as his lieutenants. Then, after lunch, we learned some entirely new stuff—weapon stuff. Knives, machetes, kama, sai...This was about the point at which we all really began to wrap our heads around the fact that we were studying a lethal art. After that, we ran the hill again and had a *second* class; and then, with the sun at rest beyond the western mountains, we built our fire.

Sensei always says the best time to practice escrima is around a bonfire at night. Maybe I'm biased, but I think he's absolutely right. The dim, shifting light and the hurtling hazard of sticks coming at your skull key up your senses to concert pitch; and once you're there, you somehow forget the sticks altogether. Bruce Lee said the highest art is no art: when you so thoroughly absorb and embody your lessons that you transcend them, and the line between will and action disappears. The same precept holds in music, poetry, dance—swimming, tennis, driving, chopping vegetables—anything you like. On a very small scale (as above, so below), it echoes the Lord's command not to prepare our arguments in advance but to make the Holy Spirit welcome in our hearts and let Him speak through us when the time for speaking comes (Luke 12:12). All these ruminations may flicker through a man's mind in the second it takes him to parry his partner's full-strength swing by firelight beneath a waxing moon; and in that second, the escrimador's art becomes a minor sacrament. Whether you eat or you drink—

After that, we ate and talked and made S'mores and finally went to bed. I must record that one of many traits my cousin and I share is a detestation of tents and camping in general. Those nights were not times of luxury for us. (Also, the hot dogs we ate that first night made several of us sick—probably because we cooked them over burning fence-posts treated with lead-based paint. Not exactly our smartest move—but a tale destined to be immortally re-told at every subsequent camp and so, I feel, well worth the transient discomfort.) The next two days were just the same, except that we visited the river in the afternoon to wash our reeking selves. But on the evening of the third day, when darkness came and we built our raging fire, the ritual commenced. We call it the Tap-Out Ceremony.

D.J. beat the drum, a simple pounding tempo, ever escalating. T. stood at attention by the fire, perfectly still. The rest of us, at Sensei's word, ran around him in circles, gradually picking up speed. Once in awhile one of us would break away from the group, sprint toward our boy, and stop at the last moment, only to return to the accelerating orbit around the central blaze. This went on and on, faster and faster, and T. stood unflinching, awaiting the Tap. Then, without warning,

Sensei came roaring out of the shadows and body-checked him so hard he went flying backward. By the time he hit the ground, Sensei had already pounced on him, blind-folded him, and dragged him away into the night.

The rest of us stood there, silent and still. It must have been five minutes before anyone ventured to speak. None of us had ever seen such a thing before. But the next time Josh and I saw it, we'd be the ones standing by the fire.

Kara

In June our lease expired at the House, and a change of regimes came about. Josh went to stay with his folks for a few weeks, an hour's drive east of Jotun. I returned to my vagrant ways. Lane moved to Burlington. (In fact, I was helping him move when I witnessed the most hair-raisingly precise instant of comedic timing I've ever seen in real life: we were pulling into the driveway of a college tenement that was in the process of being vacated and he remarked, "I wonder if we're allowed to park here?"—to which I replied with casual pugnacity, "Aw, what're they gonna do about it?" And I'd no sooner closed my mouth than some kids on the third floor shoved an old couch out the window and it came plummeting down and smashed itself to bits on the ground maybe twenty feet in front of us. We parked somewhere else.) Meanwhile, Rob and Topper were also leaving town and Sensei was looking for a new place, so he moved in and was given the Loft. Lissa stayed, and Arnold and D.J. came to dwell there as well. About this time it ceased to be merely the House and became "the Kai House."

When T. returned from his mysterious initiation, soaking wet and wearing the knightly black around his waist, Josh and I were confirmed in our driving desire to earn the same honor and stand with him as peers. That whole year—actually fourteen months—was our "black belt year," the home stretch of heightened training to prepare for our own camp the following summer. At the same time, however, we were both very broke and staggering under debts—Josh to his car company and I to our landlords at the House, to whom I now owed almost two full months' back rent. It was therefore Providential when our second cousin Donna invited us to come and paint her inn that July.

See—my dad's an only child and there are no other Toners directly related to us, so our family circle was always small. My mom and Josh's mom (Aunt Kathy) are sisters, and there's a sizeable family on that side, but for whatever reason I'd never been close with them. But we happened to be visiting Gram and Grampa that June when our mothers' cousin Donna dropped by for a visit as well. She ran a bed and breakfast in Ashfield, Massachusetts, during the fall and needed someone to scrape and re-paint the whole thing by August; and Josh and I sort of glanced at each other and shrugged and said, "We'll do it." And so it was.

That July lives in my memory as one of the most pleasant months of my life. My listeners, when I relate this particular tale, have occasionally expressed surprise that Josh and I could spend every minute together for a whole month and never bicker; but Lord, what was there to bicker about? We had a whole inn to ourselves. We rose late each day, ate copiously, and spent three or four hours painting; then we'd go swim in the lake, swing sticks at each other for awhile, and retire to watch movies all night. We ate more Chinese food and pizza than any man ever should, and drank enough soda to kill a small boar (we were up to a six-pack a day—each—when we decided we should probably cut back a little), and were still young enough that the mere abundance of junk food was a delight to our souls and no threat to our metabolisms. Donna collected antiques and the inn was stuffed with pricey-looking artifacts, so we abstained from alcohol that whole July for fear of breaking something in our rowdiness; and neither of us yet drank coffee. So, we sat in the sun (she had these great hanging chairs on the porch) and sipped our Cokes and did our job and let the world go its way without us for a time. Sensei even came down to visit us one weekend, and showed us a more advanced disarming technique than any we'd yet seen. Oh, and also there was a cat whose name I've forgotten, who used to bring us dismembered tree frogs—either in token of affection or by way of mocking our hunting skills, depending on whose version of feline psychology you listen to. I prefer to believe the former.

At month's end I turned twenty-four. Donna's brother David gave me the welcome gift of underwear; and as he observed at the time, "You know you're getting older when you get underwear and you're actually happy about it." We finished our task—satisfactorily enough, I believe—and Donna, God bless her, gave us both enough money to settle our debts and live through August without needing to seek employment. We returned to the inn twice more—once a couple of months later, to help her install insulation in the attic, and again at Thanksgiving—but eventually she sold the place, and it stands now only in our stories of the elder days.

August was a good month too. The Kai had missed us, and we now realized we'd missed the Kai. It was good to be home, even if we were both homeless. Merrin had moved away (and I'm pretty sure he still owes me twenty bucks), and Cherie was now renting a place—again, platonically—with our most excellent friend Juan. Apart from being an all-around good sort, Juan was acclaimed in our little circle for having on two separate occasions run down and apprehended shoplifters from the store where he worked. Every few years, Josh tried to interest him in studying the arts with us, but he never showed any inclination. To each his own. At any rate, we spent the rest of the summer training and wasting time with our friends—in the special sense in which the waste of time is the best possible use of it. Josh mostly crashed on Juan and Cherie's couch or in his own car; I took up residence in the old abandoned power-house by the Jotun River, dubbing it Moria. (I'm fond of giving mythic nomenclature to my various haunts. My ruined house in West Virginia was called Charn, from the Narnia books; my spot under a fenced-off bridge in Massachusetts, Trellem—a worn-down form of "troll-home.") Most evenings and well into the nights, we hung out on the deserted JSC campus with our buddies Groo and Zane, the security guards. It was during this period, this calm caesura in the long dark saga of Jotun town, that I was introduced to the music of Warren Zevon, best known for his "Werewolves of London." He soon became my favorite of all musicians, utterly and forever—indeed, I listen to him even as I write these words—and he comes into this tale again.

And...it was during this period that I met Kara. Groo's younger brother Chan had finished high school in May, and he spent a few nights up on campus with us every week. Most nights his friend Kara came along. She was in the same graduating class and a month shy of nineteen—a good deal younger than me, but rather older too. I realize that not everyone believes in such things; but if I'm to speak truth, I can only say that I loved that girl as soon as I ever saw her. She was always beautiful (although she never thought so), but beyond that there was just—*something* in her, something elvish, that glittered through her gaze and her stance and her words, that made everything in her presence seem to glow. I came in time to call it her Karaness; apart from that, I still can't put a name to it. But I didn't yet have the depth of soul to love her deeply. It was precisely by being in love with her that I came to be deepened.

It was a troubled courtship, though. The course of true love and all that, I reckon. On a merely logistical level, neither of us had a car and she lived about fifteen miles away—not an epic trek, but too far to travel casually on foot twice a day. Luckily, it turned out that she and Chan were also friends with our Kai brother Ned (another of Jotun's many overlapping destinies), and between the two of them she got into town most nights. Groo and Zane worked from 11 p.m. to 7 a.m., and we (a pronoun which can refer here to any combination of myself, Josh, Juan, Ned, Chan, and Kara) often spent the entire night kicking around campus with them; so she and I could usually contrive to slip away and talk privately for an hour or two without discourtesy to the others. We were strangely fascinated by one another from the outset—she because she'd never met a professed Catholic whose company she actually enjoyed, and I because, well, she was Kara. Turns out I don't have at my disposal a plethora of what is popularly called "game"—possibly because I can't help using words like *plethora*—and I told her pretty early on that I had feelings for her, which apparently you're not supposed to do (?). Happily, she did in fact reciprocate them, and I believe she found my bumblings endearing; but she had undertaken a resolution of sorts not to enter another romantic relationship until she could comprehend and repair a troubling flaw in her mind and heart.

I garnered the details of the matter only slowly, over months, but the gist of it was that she had a dark compulsion to turn suddenly and hurt the boys who loved her. Not for any real reason, and even against her own habitual conception of the person she wanted to be: there simply came a moment in her relationships when she would end up somehow torturing or betraying her boyfriend, and she was forever repenting and trying to "fix herself" and stop doing such things, only to find herself doing them again. I always suspected it was some manner of externalized self-destructive impulse—she came, after all, from a generation of girls many of whom I've known have expressed their personal angst by cutting themselves—but what do I know, I'm no psychologist. It probably didn't help that her parents allowed strange men to sleep over in their adolescent daughter's bedroom; I'm afraid I don't have many nice things to say about them. At all events, she was terrified of hurting or corrupting me, especially when she discovered I was a virgin, and she was constantly drawing back during the early months of our acquaintance.

Even apart from our emotional connection, however, we were kindred minds—she was my very best friend for a long time—and we kept finding our way back to each other. As the leaves began to fall, I re-took my old job at the grim little gas station outside of town and she got a job somewhere doing something I can't remember, and spent most of her free time in Jotun. (She was still living at home and hadn't yet enrolled in college.) Came a certain cool November evening by the river's edge when I at last let slip the L word, and Kara said it back, and we ceased to be just friends.

And now we're almost back to the karate part of the story. Kara enrolled at JSC in January, and moved into the dorms; and now, being a fellow Jotunite, she started making friends with my adoptive martial family. Being also an athlete and a tough chick, she decided that studying KJJ sounded like fun— and thus we came to be fellow fighters-in-training. As for so many of us, the Kai rapidly became one of the most important things in her life. And she was good, folks—she was very, very good. Furthermore, she was an extremely magnetic young woman who quickly attracted new friends on campus, and several of them joined us as well. So came Susannah, the Jewish singer who chanted the Torah at synagogue, tore things up on the grappling mat, and dated our main man Arnold for over a year (long time in those days). So came Riggs, a man of tremendous loyalty and heart, and also one of the few people even louder and sillier in public than me; we had some good times, and annoyed a fairly large number of people. So came Tim, a fellow Star Wars/Trek enthusiast, master of drunken kata and possessor of, unequivocally, the weirdest sense of humor I have ever encountered. Sensei once turned to Tim out of the blue and said, "Hey Tim, call me a tree," and when Tim said, "You're a tree," Sensei shouted, *"No, I'm not!"* The rest of us only stood there blinking in perplexity, but Tim laughed so hard he literally fell over. Like I said—to each his own.

I'd left the gas station by this time and gotten a new job up on campus washing dishes in the cafeteria (or the Church of Aramark, as Tim unaccountably called it). My co-worker was the infamous Nick the Quick, a gnomish fellow with a curious talent for knowing every single student who came up to drop off dirty dishes by their Christian names. Renee, who was very fond of Nick, was amused when she heard that I was working with him; and she was kind enough to warn me that he had a dreadful mean streak—not with people, but with silverware. I saw it soon: whenever my distinguished colleague dropped a piece of cutlery, he would shriek obscenities at it—and within a couple of weeks, I found myself struggling with the exact same habit. What could that spoon be *thinking?*

I'd also left Moria—or, more honestly, I'd been extracted by the police and rescued from vagrancy charges by Zane. (He too came to the occasional class with us, and often referred to me as Chokeymon out of my fondness for that method of concluding a grappling match.) At the dawn of '02, my official residence was a moldering pick-up truck deep in the woods near campus, in a clearing which I called the Glade of San Salvador. (As long as the windows are intact, a vehicle retains your body heat really well on winter nights.) I also frequented Juan and Cherie's couch; that's where I was on the morning of 9/11, and many of us gathered in their kitchen for mutual consolation. Josh was now teaching at a high school in Shalott,

about an hour's commute away, and drove down for the weekends and class on Mondays. He had an apartment with a
co-worker, but when in Jotun he stayed in a curtained-off corner
bed in the Loft that Lissa dubbed the Nest. In fact, we often
shared it; we'd been sharing beds since our summers at the
farm as small children and thought nothing of it, although we
were affectionate enough that outsiders *constantly* assumed
we were gay.

Around this time, Sensei's younger brother Craig joined
the Kai—or rather, re-joined it. Like T., he'd been a part of the
old guard before Lane and I ever set foot in the dojo back in
Stowe, and had learned a great deal. He'd left the arts a few
years earlier, and Josh and I hadn't even met him—he was a
chef like his brother, and kept himself awfully busy—but he was
reaching a point in his life where he needed some kind of a
purpose, and God knows the Kai had given that to many others
before him. He was a wiry sumbitch, and he and I had some
highly challenging matches. In '03, Craig became a *sho-dan*—
the last one we would produce for over half a decade. But I'm
getting ahead of the story.

Class went on through the winter. People came and went,
but over time a staunch core of at least a dozen of us was
found to persevere. We learned and evolved, both individually
and familially, and grew ever closer. Every Monday after class
we all went to the Mo-Vegas McDonald's for a late supper and
then back to the Kai House to hang out. And most weekends

we threw those endless parties, though they were smaller now than in 2000, often composed only of our own group and immediate friends. The bond between me and Kara grew more powerful and profound with the passing days. And she, for her part, developed swiftly as a martial artist. One night at a Kai party, we had a visitor who was either amused or threatened by the idea of a girl who could handily defeat him in personal combat; and under that tiresome guise of "just kiddin' around," he kept throwing punches at her, stopping an inch from her face, and saying, "What would you do if I did this?" Finally, she parried his arm, popped him in the jaw, and head-twisted him right to his back on the carpet, and said, "I'd do *that*."

Man—if there was ever a moment that made you want to nudge the guy next to you and go, "That right there? That's my girl."

Black Belts!

As our fair Lord tells us, "Those who are faithful in small matters will be trusted with great ones" (Luke 16:10). In KJJ, a slowly increasing mastery of the basics enables the practitioner to ascend to ever more direct, efficient, as it were pure techniques: the expert can safely utilize shortcuts that would stunt the apprentice. Thus, the final disarm—after you've grasped a complicated series of preliminary moves—is simply to smash your enemy's hand with a stick. (So, why the preliminaries? Firstly, to give you something to fall back on if the enemy foils your direct attack; secondly, to teach your body to move and your mind to grasp the elemental kinesthetics of the art, such as angles of attack and the all-important footwork.) These ultimate mysteries now began to unveil themselves. And as spring rolled around again, we left the dojo and resumed our training in the grass and the dirt.

For me and Josh, it was the last push to camp. We now handled a lot of the teaching—since that's really what it means to be a master—especially Josh, who would go on to become one of the youngest school principals in Vermont. From the timid kid who used to get pushed around by his girlfriends, he had not so much blossomed as erupted these past two years. I lacked the knack for switching off the relaxed attitude we all had with each other outside of class (though I won't pretend there wasn't a social pecking order among us, conforming with only a few variations of personality to our rank structure); most of the drill-sergeant stuff fell to Josh. Some of the *kyu* ranks were sort of "Monday martial artists," training only three hours a week and neglecting to practice their skills the rest of the time. We almost all lived within about a mile of each other, and the serious students often got together during the week— either with T. and myself or in groups of juniors running drills by themselves—to hone what we learned on Mondays. Josh was constantly pushing the less serious ones to commit themselves. "Use not vain repetition as the heathen do" (Matthew 6:7): whether you're praying your rosary or hammering your katas, you only get out what you put in. Needless to say, the same applies to the study of physics, taxidermy, ophthalmology, or what have you—but *this* book is about the martial arts. Let the ophthalmologists write their own memoirs.

When new students came to class, particularly big guys with a belligerent streak, as not infrequently occurred, it was my job to grapple them. Sensei wanted them quickly submitted, and not by himself, to demonstrate the efficacy of what he taught. I loved my job, and I definitely let it go to my head; we'll get to that in a moment. Josh's job was harder. He was the rag doll for the humbler students who were still learning to control their movements on the mat; he let them throw him around, flop all over him, and usually catch him with all kinds of knees and elbows and head-butts, totally by accident and often without even noticing when it happened, and he generally let them submit him once they'd managed a few successful escapes and transitions. No less than when we'd first begun, aspirin and zheng-gu-shui remained our constant allies.

Sensei once taught us about the Japanese concept of *hara*, or "one-point"—the single point of perfect focus that a martial artist strives to achieve in which pain, fear, and distraction become meaningless. Josh used to call it his "worm-point" because he typically found it when he was face-first in the turf. Interestingly, the word literally means simply, "stomach"—much as we get "courage" from *couer*, "heart." It's the root of the term *hara-kiri*, "stomach-cut," the samurai's ritual self-disembowelment (chronically mispronounced by Americans as "Harry Caray," the baseball announcer). I suppose we could translate it "guts," but that lacks a certain poetry. For the two of us, those early months of '02 were an ongoing pursuit of *hara*.

My balance, my equipoise, my one-point, failed me twice in this period—once by an excess of pride and once, I think,

89

by a dearth of it. The first time was in class. I hadn't grappled Sensei in a couple of years, and I asked him for a match, which he granted. It started off friendly enough, but he very quickly caught me with a gi-choke to which I should have tapped immediately. Some part of me rebelled against such a defeat, and I took the thing straight to a level of intensity reserved for life-and-death situations. And he *could* have ended the match— by killing me. As he was not prepared to rupture his friend's carotid arteries for no reason at all, however, he had to fall back on auxiliary strategies for which I was prepared, and I "won" the match. The room was silent. Everyone had felt the energy in that fight—the darkness, the wrongness of it. I felt it too, once the adrenaline wore off; and when Sensei and I talked after class, I suddenly found myself crying. He was kind about it, and we only ever spoke of that day one other time; I think he understood that all he could really do was wait for my ego to burn itself out.

At the same time, on the other hand, I was gradually becoming aware of a deep sense of insecurity in my relationship with Kara. For one thing, she was a college student and aspiring psychotherapist—bright, charismatic, and lovely as the evening stars—and I washed dishes and slept in a deserted truck. She was young enough to look past such things for now, but that's because the possibility of marriage had never crossed her mind before. It came in with the other ground of my insecurity: the question of sex. Kara had no religious formation to speak of, and God knows there's nothing in secular culture to encourage the idea of chastity among young people. We had discussed the matter early on and she'd been willing to try waiting on a sort of "we'll see what happens" basis. Her assumption, as she told me much later, was that I'd cave in before too long and the conflict would resolve itself without trouble. When that didn't happen, and the months began to pass, we discussed the matter again. And then again, and again and again and again. (To this day it drives me right to the crumbling brink of psychosis when people say that *guys* are only after sex.) Finally one afternoon I lost all semblance of sense and flatly broke up with her on the spot. To my mind, the thing had been building toward explosion for some time; to Kara, it came totally out of the blue. It was far from the last time I would make a mess of things with her—our little saga had barely even started.

Still, I feel like we were both fairly "mature" about the whole thing (I guess that's the relevant adjective): we managed to co-exist with minimal drama in the Kai and our still-growing circle of mutual friends, at least for the nonce. Soon May rolled around and JSC let out for the summer, and I was out of a job. Since my meals had always been free and I had no living expenses, I'd saved up plenty of money, and I now used it to support myself as I entered the most intensive training I have ever undergone. Because I'm a huge dork, I called it "Vegeta training" (accent on the second syllable, pronounced "jeet"), after a particularly driven character in Dragonball Z. Josh had two or three weeks of teaching left in Shalott, as college generally lets out before high school, so I spent my days alone in the Glade of San Salvador just murdering myself—one-handed push-ups with a log balanced on my back, wind-sprints through the forest with heavy jugs in either hand, a hundred flying spin-kicks per leg as a basic stretch, and of course my daily regimen on the Tree of Woe. This was a gnarled old oak that I would climb to the top of, so that I was in real danger of injury if I fell (the idea was to tap hidden reservoirs of qi through fear and pain), and then hang upside down by my legs and do abdominal crunches. The wood cut into my shins so deeply that I carried the marks for months afterward; that was an added bonus I picked up from observing the Thai kick-boxers, who toughen their shin-bones by repeated trauma to create a harder kicking surface. I used to wonder in some clinical part of my brain, as I cranked those crunches of woe, if any hikers or homesteaders were close enough to hear me screaming my soul out, and what they might think if they saw me; but no one ever did. Just as well I never got hurt, you might well say. And I honestly can't remember now if that ever occurred to me at the time. All I can say is, I've been kept safe through so many damn fool misadventures over the years that if I hadn't already believed in guardian angels at the outset, I surely would by now.

But there's only so much crazy you can do by yourself. When Josh's summer finally began, we brought things to a new order of magnitude: grappling, stick drills, marathon katas, "planting rice" the length of the soccer fields (dropping to a full crouch and springing back up to cover about a quarter of a foot each time), and the inevitable roundhouse kicks to one another's quadriceps to build toughness. *Good times.* By July we were, beyond all question, in the best shape of our lives and half-insane with readiness for camp. Yet we did more than martial arts during those weeks.

Josh, for his part, took the role of Lysander in a community theater production of *A Midsummer Night's Dream*. It was there that we first met the young lady (merrily wandering the midsummer night as Robin Goodfellow) who would ultimately ace the Returning Cousin Test of half-forgotten lore. Miranda's her name, true sister of my heart—but at the time they perceived each other only as friends and fellow cast-members, and none of us had the faintest clue of what was to come. (There's a dash of Puck in the Divine Nature, I sometimes think.) I tagged along to rehearsals occasionally, but I also spent a good deal of time gallivanting with our boy Riggs. We were a reliably bad influence on each other, and it wouldn't do to stay out of *all* trouble in the smoldering shadows of June. Thus I came to meet John the rugger (the bench press dude I mentioned earlier), as Riggs was the sort of person who seems to know everybody.

As things fell out, Kara was now dating John, and living at his campus apartment. Now, I had always hitherto believed that we of the Kai were pretty hard drinkers—but that was before I started partying with the rugby team. Man, those guys drank. Josh and I frankly earned our place among them by our fluency in their language of violent rough-housing (and I'll never forget old Brad, whom I'd just amicably beaten up, consoling himself by bodily tearing a nearby stop sign right out of the earth); after that, he and Riggs and I spent a great many nights there. Kara and I were trying hard to be friends, which was complicated by the fact that we were still head over heels in love—not that either of us admitted as much to ourselves. I briefly dated her friend Fae during this time, insisting to my own heart that I was over Kara altogether.

Fae was. . . well. . . she was Fae. I'd really need another whole book to do her justice. We couldn't converse for five minutes without cross-purposes (she was a hardened atheist), but whenever we were quiet together, the spirits pelted us with luminous things. A dark field came alight with fireflies, a spill of water from a dam caught a sunbeam and burst into rainbows— this is another part of the story I must understate for fear of being suspected of hyperbole. But she was a keen mind, and figured out sooner than I did that Kara and I were not finished yet. Drama would soon ensue, but the telling must await the next chapter. Black belt camp came first.

Ah, camp. *Camp!* By this time there was over a score of us there. T.'s camp was three days; for me and Josh, it was four. (For Lissa and Craig the next year, it was five. I can't say I regret that it never got any longer.) The particulars of the camp were mostly the same as the year before, but the whole experience was immensely heightened for me and Josh by the fact that it was *our* camp, *our* trial, *our* crucible. Also, this year Sensei came up with the idea of putting us in groups when the day's work was done and we were gathered by the fire at night, and giving us koans to act out. The only one I remember is the old tale of the mouse to whom the gods keep granting the wish to be as strong as something else—the sun, the cloud, the wind, and the wall—only to find in the end that the strength of the wall is surpassed by the might of the mouse. It's basically a transcendental game of rock-paper-scissors, but the rendition at camp stays in my memory because every time Ned (the mouse) wished to become something else, Tim (the gods—I guess?) would say, "And so you shall!" in a screeching falsetto and smack him on the head with a magic wand made of escrima stick. Everything's funnier anyway, when you're that tired; their performance nearly killed us all.

The time for the Tap-Out Ceremony came. We lit the great fire. Josh and I stood side by side. D.J. beat the drums. The others stood around us in a ring. And Sensei and T. began to run, to run in circles around the fire and dart toward us and stop and circle and accelerate and dart and stop and circle and accelerate again. The cicadas sang. The bonfire blazed. And then Sensei darted at Josh and didn't stop, and I could feel the impact from a foot away and my cousin went hurtling backward, and then T. came charging at me and this time I didn't feel the impact at all. And they blind-folded us and dragged us away to the secret initiation which I am sworn never to reveal.

When we returned, we were *sho-dan*.

Gotterdamerung

Sensei was even more right than he knew. "Now you are ready to begin," he told us, once we'd belted up. I had barely even come far enough to perceive how far there truly was to go. Looking back now—and it feels like peering through the wrack of centuries, not years—I always think of Alexander Pope's line about the foolish young mountaineer who thinks he's conquered the Alpine heights until he gets high enough to see the *real* heights: "Hills peep o'er hills, and Alps on Alps arise!"

A few days later (once we'd all regained the use of our limbs), we held the giant party at T.'s place. He and I have almost the same birthday, so we were celebrating that joint occasion as well as the ascension of Josh and myself to black belt status: at least four parties' worth of revelry rolled into one, and I daresay we did them full justice. It was during these festivities that Lissa, Josh, and I decided to take a road trip (everything seems like a good idea at a party; apparently the ancient Persians debated everything twice, once drunk and once sober). None of us had been to Seattle, and Lissa had a cousin out there—and more to the point, she'd never experienced the "road trip" trope of some of our better tales, and wanted to try it at least once. So we laid plans to take off in Josh's Impala, Seamus, in a couple of weeks.

For my part, another motive soon became extant in my fevered little mind. Since the dawn of 1996, I'd been bouncing around the country after some nebulous vision of a heroic destiny, and I'd never lost the sense of being led (or *driven*) until I joined the Kai. At the time—somehow—I failed to discern that this might be an indication of the Holy Spirit wanting me to stay put for awhile. I simply assumed my sense of the numinous had gone on the fritz. Accordingly, I'd stayed in Jotun until I got my belt—but now, I thought, perhaps it was time to go back on the road. I had nothing in particular to keep me here: no job, no girl, no home. So I decided that when Josh and Lissa returned to Vermont, I'd remain behind in Washington State. I had plenty of time to say goodbye to my kindred of the Kai, and everyone supported me and wished me the best. There was only one complication.

Right about this time, in the general passion of camp and imminent departure, I found myself confessing my undiminished feelings to Kara—and she replied in kind. Problem was, she was still living with John, who was totally crazy about her.

Fae and I had already "sort of" terminated our "sort of" relationship, partly because she refused to believe I was over Kara (rightly, as it turned out) and partly because of the sex thing again. Our friendship was not the only one to be mangled during this whole debacle. To her credit, Kara told John upfront how she felt about me, but he begged her to stay with him at least for a little while and re-consider. So—I decided to go ahead with my plans to stay in Seattle, and give them a chance. John was a good man, and ultimately got the worst deal of any of us. Maybe the most crucial trait shared by me and Kara was that we both *wanted* to be good people; but we hadn't yet grasped that the only path to that peak is self-sacrifice.

There's something cleansing about a road trip. Whatever regrets may lie behind or fears before you, their talons are withheld while you traverse the void between. "You are not the same people who left that station / Or who will arrive at any terminus" (T. S. Eliot, "The Dry Salvages"). It's a long way overland from one end of North America to the other, and Josh and Lissa did all the driving (my license was expired), so I got to see a lot of the northern bread-basket. My only really tale-worthy memory of the trek west is of a rest stop in South Dakota where we did all our katas together on the verge of a great calm lake under a vast lowering dusk.

We spent two or three days with Lissa's cousin Gail—nice young lady—and then my comrades put the Pacific Northwest in their rear-view and headed for home. At this time I finally

earned my hobo's merit badge by sneaking into a train-yard
and hopping a north-bound freight. I visited Everett and Bell-
ingham, saw a very cool '50s-style McDonald's, filled a notebook with love poetry for Kara, and unfortunately lost my bali-
song (butterfly knife). The area seemed very friendly to the
homeless—I actually saw a dude in a sleeping bag on the lawn
of a bank at eleven o'clock on a weekday morning in Seattle—
but of course this was ten years ago, so I wouldn't offer that
as a contemporary tip for the aspiring vagrant. In fact, frankly,
I really don't recommend vagrancy at all if you can avoid it. It's
got its upsides, but you have to weigh them against the ever-
present threat of rape. I've been the target of would-be preda-
tors on three separate occasions over the years; thank God I
never got ganged up on, or blind-sided, or caught sleeping or
drunk. There's better ways to see the country—but, again, to
each his own.

I don't exactly recall, but I believe I was only out there for
a fortnight or maybe three weeks. The thought of Kara called
me home—insofar as the word *home* applies to someone like
me. With the very dregs of my funds I bought a Greyhound
ticket and headed east, back across the great reaches of the
continent. (On that bus I went three days without food. Interesting experience.) When I returned, JSC was back in session
and I got my old dishwashing gig back. It was a strange time:
Riggs and Susannah (she of the Torah-singing) were working
in the kitchen too, making pizzas for on-campus delivery in the

evenings—and then John and Kara also took jobs there, as delivery-people. Poor John. We liked each other a lot—but how could we help hating each other? I remember saying once how I wished we hadn't both fallen for this girl, and his reply: "But we both know that's impossible."

By this time, Kara had moved back into the dorms. Around the ides of the month—actually on the same day as my parents' anniversary, oddly enough—she turned twenty, and at last made her choice between suitors. John didn't take it too well (no more would I have done, if she'd chosen differently); he tried to go on being friends with us, but it was painful for him, and I didn't see much of him afterward. I stayed in Kara's room fairly often once our re-union became official, but as winter came creeping onto the calendars again, I decided—not, I'll allow, without some prompting—it was time to get my own place. After a couple months of once again working steadily with no bills for bed or board, I'd saved up plenty to get a spot in an apartment building known as "the Jotun ghetto." (My cousin Sarah had lived there the year before, in a room whose floor was so uneven you could literally put a marble in one corner and watch it roll across to the other.) This dwelling, I dubbed "Winter Hall." And it was there that I at last made a choice of my own.

As I write this, I'm single and have no particular prospects for further romance. But if I ever do end up married, there will be one gift I can no longer give my wife. My mind, my body, my heart—my work, my devotion, my faith, hope, and love—all these

I can give. But not my virginity. Not the knowledge that she's the only one there's ever been. When spring semester of '03 rolled around, she left the dorms and moved into Winter Hall.

Meanwhile, it was black belt year for Craig and Lissa. With the coming of the snows, we were back in the ski-lodge dojo (for the last time). Josh and I weren't allowed to rest long on our laurels: increasingly, the burden of teaching fell to us as the newest black belts. Kara's older sister Jill joined us around this time, and she and Josh ended up dating—thus putting an end to his lengthy interregnum between queens. And then! After three years together, Sensei put an engagement ring on Lissa's finger. The date was set for early autumn, and it got me thinking. This love of mine, this love of my life: what was I to do with our mingled fates? Could I marry her, father children, live out a squalid existence in the bent-floored ghettoes of Jotun town scrubbing dishes? Could I offer nothing better, nothing more?

Then, as has so often happened to me (and probably happens to everyone), Providence smashed me over the head with instructions on the next step of the way. My dad never ceased to, to—let's see, we'll say politely, to *importune* me about going back to school. And early in '03, he sent me a clipping about an essay contest for a college scholarship—a three to five page essay on a saint of our choice, for the Thomas Merton College of Liberal Arts in New Hampshire. I had no real interest in the school, but I decided to crack my knuckles and take a stab at the essay just for the heck of it—and I won a thousand dollars off the tuition costs. (Wrote about St. Francis, of course.) Which got me thinking again—what is it that grown-ups, those elusive creatures of fable and shadow, do to make better lives for themselves and their families? Well heck, they go to college! I talked to Kara about it, and she supported the idea and helped me with the forms for loans and admissions and so forth. Soon it was settled that I would be off to TMC in September.

In April I got in another fight. I mention it only because it illuminated many principles for me. First, we have a rule called the escalation curve that governs appropriate levels of force-response. The severity of your enemy's attack determines the point at which you're morally justified in causing temporary pain, permanent injury, or (God forbid) death. Kara and I were walking down the street minding our own business when some jerk in a pick-up truck drove by and yelled something unprintable at my girl—so naturally, I took off running after him. I'm pretty fast, and there was some traffic, and I kept him in view down the road and around a bend and a little ways up the hill beyond. And he pulled over. My only thought was to demand an apology: technically, the appropriate response within escalation parameters, words answered with words. But this guy, an old redneck bruiser type, had seen me in his mirrors and decided to teach a lesson to the little punk who tried to chase him through his own town. (For years afterward I used to say that I once ran down a speeding truck on foot—obviously not even remotely true.) I demanded my apology, and he said more unprintable things, and we went at it.

The incident highlighted for me the significance of fighter's courtesy, which allows a framework as of friendship among men who are not yet personally acquainted. (It's more important in warrior cultures—the samurai, the Vikings, the feudal knights—than in "civilized" societies, of course. Mouth off to an ancient Athenian and you'll probably get an intellectual trouncing and walk away looking like a moron, but at least you'll walk away. Try it with a samurai and your body is liable to go wandering off with an arterial geyser where your head used to be.) It also taught me first-hand that what they say in the war movies is true: an enemy with the high ground does have a serious tactical advantage. But it gave me the chance to field-test my favorite block, the moveable elbow, a stream-lined version of kung-fu hand-trapping, which worked like a *charm*. And finally, it taught me that I was a damned fool. I eventually got reverse mount on the guy and was in the process of choking him out, when someone started kicking me in the head. Yeah, his girl-friend was riding shotgun. I've never hit a woman—*not* because I don't consider them worthy and formidable adversaries, but simply because I've never been in enough danger from one to overcome the natural reluctance to do so. I let her man go and backed off, and we all shouted at each other until someone came out of a nearby house threatening to call the cops. At that point I just turned and walked away—and felt the flakes of enamel in my mouth from the eye-tooth which is still very slightly chipped to this day. About that time I began to come to my senses and wonder what would've happened if the guy had been driving around with two or three friends, or a knife, or a gun. I learned a great deal that day.

Alas, folks, not enough. Not yet did I have wisdom. Barely a month later, Riggs and I drank too much and did one of the dumbest things we'd done yet. We meant no harm, no meanness—that's the most I can say in our defense—we were just trying to have some goofy sophomoric fun. But the people of Jotun saw things differently when we spray-painted our Christian names on the newly re-opened bridge, damaged by snow in the winter. We were never caught, but Sensei demoted both of us for our immaturity. Riggs lost a lost few ranks of *kyu* and I was busted down to brown. It's like an allegory for my whole life.

That's how matters stood when camp came again. As I said before, it was a long one. We managed to talk Sensei into letting us drive out to Hardwick to visit the summer ice cream stand a couple of times; and also, we did knife-grappling. Not with real knives, obviously—just short dowels. Rather than starting on our feet, we'd enter the match sitting back to back and Sensei would place the "knife" in between us. Then, at the traditional Japanese cry of "Get it on!" we'd commence the mad scramble. It changed the whole dynamic. Getting to the knife before your opponent was *everything*. (I can't add much to famous street-fighter Marc "Animal" MacYoung's one rule for a knife-fight: don't get in a knife-fight.) The whole grueling week went on much as it had the last two years; but this time, the day before the Tap-Out, the black belt council and the two candidates pulled me aside for a pretty serious talk. I'd lost my temper in a match with a *kyu* rank (although he *was* eagle-clawing my larynx, which can kill a man), and nobody was happy with me. The fight with the truck guy, the spray-painting, my whole cockamamie attitude—Sensei wanted to restore my black, but he needed to be sure I wouldn't disgrace the belt. But all I could say was, "This is the only thing I've ever been a part of." I will never forget all my friends—my family—looking at each other, and then at me, and seeing nothing in their eyes but love. I'm not sure I deserved what happened next; but sometimes you just have to accept your gifts. "Lord, I am not worthy to receive You—but only say the word, and I shall be healed." The next night, I was *sho-dan* once more.

The ceremony was the same. But Josh and I, who had seen it once as *kyu* ranks and once as candidates, now saw it as senior instructors. When T. tapped out Lissa, I was the one who caught her. Sensei tapped Craig, and Josh caught him. And now we were six. The Kai was stronger, more solid, than it had ever been before. At the end of the summer, Sensei and Lissa got married. Josh moved away to Essex to be closer to his job. I went off to college in New Hampshire. And the unraveling began.

THREE

The Sword and the Cross

PART 3

Death of a Crow

Our dear Lord is not always subtle, as I've pointed out before. And it's interesting that, while omens can be either good or bad, the adjective form of the word—*ominous*—is never taken as anything but bad. My first week at Thomas More College was overwhelmingly ominous.

It started before I even set foot on campus, in fact. Riggs was kind enough to drive me down—or, at any rate, to attempt to do so. In actuality, we got about halfway there and then his radiator exploded. We called our buddy Marek, who was in turn kind enough to come find us and complete the delivery of myself to Nashua; but being in a hurry to finish the errand and go home, he was pulled over doing ninety, *and* the officer was so perspicacious as to find the open can of beer that Riggs was unwisely nursing in the shotgun seat. Marek ended up having to drive back to New Hampshire for court the next month, and they essentially banished him from the state, as far as automotive privileges went. They wouldn't even let him drive himself home.

After that doom-fraught voyage, I found myself on a tiny cloistered campus, ringed by trees and tucked away from the world. It would have been lovely in my sight if I hadn't been nurturing an irrational grudge against it for taking me away from Kara. When I wandered into the cafeteria, I happened to run into the founder and president, Dr. Sambo, who blew my mind by knowing who I was. I hadn't heard the phrase "Jim Toner's boy" since leaving Northfield at the age of twelve, but this cat placed me instantly from having been Dad's history teacher at St. Ambrose College thirty years earlier. I mean, obviously he knew in advance that I was coming, as the freshman class was only twenty-odd people (there were fewer than ninety students at the entire school), but it was still impressive. I suppose that was more auspicious than ominous. But then I went to my dorm room and found that the door didn't work.

There were only two dorms: one for the boys and one for the girls. And not only was a traditional morality assumed, but each gender was actively forbidden to set foot in the other's building. I go back and forth on whether the wholesale prohibition might have been a trifle excessive, but it was certainly effective in curtailing hanky-panky. There were no locks on the doors; we were expected to honor the Commandments and to respect one another's space. My door, however, had a faulty latching mechanism. Perhaps I should say it worked *too* well, in the sense of keeping people from entering the room—but it failed to make an exception for the legitimate residents. I have sort of a history of kicking doors in, and I was in such a mood that I didn't tinker long with the knob before simply taking a heel to the recalcitrant portal. Usually that kind of impulse gets me into unnecessary trouble, but in this case it turned out to be the only way to enter the room—although you could open the door normally from the inside—and we kicked in our way every day for the whole semester. When I met my roommate Sam, the first thing I ever said to him was, "Hey, lemme show you how to work our door." (As I write these words, eight years later, I'm in Sam's living room listening to Van Halen and drinking more coffee than can possibly bode well for my life expectancy. Several of my very best friends in this world are people I met at TMC—but of course one doesn't know such things at the time.)

The portents grew stronger and stranger. On the day that classes began—September 7th, 2003—Warren Zevon passed away. To get a sense of what this news felt like, simply go to Youtube and listen to "Keep Me In Your Heart," bearing in mind that he recorded it two weeks before leaving us. I generally draw a sharp distinction between the admiration of art and the adulation of artists, but Warren was one man I had always hoped to meet someday, and ideally get drunk with. I missed that chance; but when, God willing, our paths finally cross in the Inn at the End of the World, the first round's definitely on me. My only tribute to the man whose work has meant so much

to me is a sonnet called "The Wind" that I wrote several weeks
later:

Our songs adorn a thousand dusty shelves,
Our bones the stone of countless nameless crypts;
Our songs—we didn't write them for ourselves,
But will they still live on through others' lips?
In world's-end catacombs the poet delves,
In ghoul-dens and in Balrog-haunted deeps,
In search of angel-music, laughing elves,
And words of hope to brighten souls that weep.
Who hears us? Who is better for our toil?
Who takes our words as glowing dreams to sleep?
Who plants our hard-won songs in spirit-soil
And lets strange truths to wild fruition leap?
Enough of this. Our songs are heard, my friend—
Our voices sing forever in the wind.

The culmination came a few days after that. Apart from the
dorms, TMC has only three more structures: the "white house,"
which quarters the administrative functions; the library, whose
upper floor doubles as a brace of classrooms; and the "red
building" (I know, imaginative names, right?) which houses
both the chapel and the cafeteria as well as a few more classrooms. Between the white and the red lies the diminutive quad,
and off to your left, as you approach the chapel, is a little grotto

in the woods where Our Lady keeps a quiet watch. As I was crossing the quad early one afternoon, a fellow called Ethan came out of the cafeteria holding an injured crow.

Apparently the poor bird had gotten stuck inside somehow and had been trying to crawl out through a vent, but succeeded only in twisting his neck. His head sat crooked on his wing, and he didn't move except to cast his eyes on us as if trying to decide whether we could be trusted. We didn't quite know what to do with him, so Ethan brought him to the tree-line and set him down. We had vaguely hoped that he might only be scared, and would revive if we left him alone; but when I checked on him shortly after, he was just sitting there in the grass beneath the shadows of the leaves, silent. So—I picked him up and brought him to the grotto and sat with him under the statue of Mary. We sat there for an hour or so, and then he very quietly died in my hands, and I buried him in the soft earth at her feet. I'm conscious of having a tendency to read too much into things, but it was pretty hard not to perceive a message that my old life was soon to be likewise interred.

Sure enough, October was still young when I started getting emails from my friends back in J-town. Word on the street was, my fair Kara was sleeping with some other dude. I can't clearly say what this news did to me. Certainly, I refused to believe it right away. I called her up, and she denied it, and that was an end of the matter. In theory. Problem was, our history was a bit messier than I've set forth in these pages. I had betrayed her with Fae just a few months earlier, and she was constantly stressed out about my habitual vagrancy, and the people around us had all suffered from our shifting loyalties and affections. Poor John almost shot himself that night on the soccer field. We had passion but no charity to speak of, and that made it hard to be trusting. The suspicion prowled my heart day and night, and I finally learned what it felt like to be truly miserable. I'd suffered before, obviously, but never so deeply and never for so long. I found myself walking the streets of Nashua by night, as if I were back in 'Bama, lost in limbo. But this time I wasn't merely lost, I was tormented—so agonized in soul that it spilled over into my body and shook me like a fever. I'd done a lot of things unworthy of true love; but I loved her all the same, and I believe that on some level I already knew we weren't going to pass through this trial with our shared heart intact. Maybe this was the largely self-inflicted evil through which God chose to work the death of my callow and complacent self-will. I was definitely aware of realities more profound than a given moment's gratification by the time it was over. By Thanksgiving I was practically begging her to just tell me she was screwing other guys and get it over with, but she wouldn't make it so easy on me. It wasn't till April, when I went to visit her and actually found her in bed with another man, that I was finally freed from the crucible of doubt. But we're not quite there yet.

Josh came and got me for Thanksgiving break, and we went to Massachusetts. Grampa was dying. Mom and Dad and Josh's folks were there, and so was my oldest brother Chris. (Pat had come up a week or so earlier and we unfortunately missed him.) We had a couple of days to say goodbye. He wasn't always lucid, but he knew well enough that his family was with him, and that we love him forever. Josh and I parted again soon afterward, and our dads headed for home as well. Kathy and Mom sent us word very shortly thereafter that their father had passed away. For sixty years George and Madge Pixley were husband and wife. She survived him for a few years, and then followed him peacefully when her time came. May their souls, and the souls of all the faithful departed, through the mercy of God, rest in peace.

Meanwhile, my whole cosmos was coming apart at the seams. Everything seemed to move in extreme slow motion, and the weeks went by like millennia. Yet somehow in the middle of it all, I was bombarded with enough grace that some of it actually sank in despite myself, though it took awhile before I registered the fact. For one thing, I met the boys. Sam was a senior that year, and I was blessed to be flung into friendship with him; had we not been roommates, we might never have gotten to know each other. But I also got to know four fellow freshmen—Smiles, J.K., Luke, and Murtaugh. In time we became known as the Conclave, and we had some extraordinarily good times together. I was also surrounded by truly good and, in some cases, I believe, genuinely holy Christian people for the first time in—hell, ever, I guess. And, too, I found myself going to Mass regularly. All this, quite unbeknownst to me at the time, was irradiating my parched spirit with new life. It's odd: my memories of TMC are extremely happy ones, even though I was in a frenzy of despair all the while. My weeds were being uprooted, my hoarded grain falling to the earth to bring forth fruit. I take it there's no way for this to happen without suffering, or Jesus Himself would not have been called a Man of Sorrows. But of course, that particular insight comes from a sternly inculcated sense of perspective, absent by definition from someone being forced to grow up.

I spent Christmas break with Josh and Marek in Essex. Kara said she needed space, so I didn't see her at all. By the time I got back to TMC, I'd begun at long last to allow myself to be angry about the whole wretched debacle. First semester, I actually got mostly A's; second semester, I believe I tanked every class. (Never did bother picking up my final report card.) Up till then, I'd been clinging to the hope of a future with Kara, a job and a dog and a white fence and so forth: as the dream withered, so did my involvement in higher education. The irony is, I still learned a tremendous amount at TMC—about poetry and philosophy and the Faith, and about the daily behavior of people earnestly endeavoring to live virtuous lives. Apparently it looks a great deal like normal life in all externals: you still study, eat junk food, make silly jokes, watch TV, listen to music, go jogging, even smoke and drink too much occasionally (the academic atmosphere at TMC got pretty high stress at times);

but on some often unconscious level, you're always holding open the door of your heart to let the Christ-light in. After awhile it becomes more something you are than something you do. "The highest art is no art." All the rules and rubrics a good Christian finds himself following seem to be in the nature of training wheels: to be mastered in order that we might transcend them. "I come not to destroy the Law but to fulfill it" (Matthew 5:17). Ultimately what transfigures the soul isn't *our* actions—although good behavior flows naturally from love—it's the living relationship with Jesus of Nazareth. All of this I began to process only very gradually, over the next several years. In the meantime I was turning in a wholly execrable scholastic performance.

Second semester I was roommates with J.K., and he calmly took it upon himself to keep me from disintegrating altogether. I remember he would actually keep pre-tied ties in the closet for me to make sure I was ready for Mass, and he always managed to smuggle food out of the cafeteria in case I missed mealtimes. Altogether I had such loving friends taking care of me during this nightmarish time that it reminds me of the old story about God and the footprints in the sand. I also grew closer with some folks outside the Conclave, who would be embarrassed to be described as profoundly beautiful and magical people but cannot with accuracy be described in any other way. There was our friend Leah, an honorary Conclavian, who once found me drunk on a rooftop; fellow tree-climber Kateri, who gave me a

Miraculous Medal on a night when I was a hair's breadth from running berserk; and, of course, Annabelle. Anna was a philosophy major in her senior year (and an aikido student!), and the most *incarnational* person I've ever met. By that I mean that the line between matter and mind seemed almost preternaturally hazy in her being, and ideas affected her like physical events. I've seen her light up like a kid at Christmas over a metaphysical theorem, and we once nearly had a screaming match about the logical ramifications of time travel. There was no such thing as a dull discussion with Anna. And it was she who taught me—simply by being Annabelle—what it means to be truly in love with Our Lord. I'd always grasped in principle that the Truth is not a thing or a thought but a Person, but I hadn't quite gotten it into my heart that the joy of this one great desiring, of which all our mortal desires are but echoes, is better expressed by laughing or fighting or weeping or dancing than by mere cerebration (though there's a time for that too). She taught me what it was like to be someone for whom theology was not a set of formulae but a warm, breathing reality. For me, she enacted the old maxim of St. Francis: "Preach the Gospel always. Use words when necessary."

By April, the relationship between me and Kara was already dead in my mind and heart. She would hardly talk to me, yet she wouldn't end the thing and free me, and I lacked the strength of character to end it myself. I don't know what was happening inside of her during this time, and she's not here to give her side of the story, so I'll keep the account brief. As I mentioned earlier, I went home for Easter and found her with another guy, and that was it. At the time, all I felt was relief; but that was only the system shock of a rapid, efficient amputation. The pain and debilitation would catch up with me later. It was a long, long, long Good Friday before my rock rolled away. Oh—and to anticipate the question I usually get when I relate this incident to a male audience, "What did you do to the guy?"—I didn't do anything to him. I didn't even know the poor shmuck. My quarrel wasn't with him. I said goodbye to my erstwhile *raison d'être* and I walked away. Well, okay, actually I said some pretty horrible things and threw a giant rock at her car, and *then* I walked away. Didn't speak to her for most of a year after that, nor see her till tag-end 2007—and not again after that until 2011.

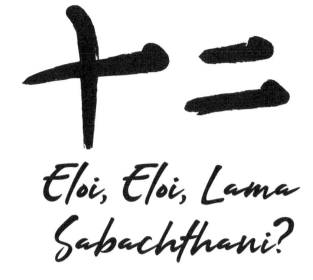

Eloi, Eloi, Lama Sabachthani?

Maybe it's just playing with words, but I have sometimes thought that you don't truly begin to see people until you begin to love them—which means that all true love is love at first sight. The first time I saw Annabelle, we'd been casually acquainted for months, but I'd been too absorbed with my own travail to perceive her most salient characteristic: the halo. Speaking now with clinical detachment, long after the fact, I can authoritatively corroborate the impression of that dazzled Toner past who thought if ever a daughter of men could be mistaken for an angel of God, it was she. It was like emerging from the gloom of an endless midnight into a sudden dawn in which the sun not only shone but danced as at Fatima.

Every year at TMC, the sophomore class spent the entire spring semester in Rome; so the campus' already sparse population thinned even more, and the seniors were mostly given their own dorm rooms. One evening in early May, I swung by Sam's room in the basement to see what mischief he was up to, and he admitted me to his subterranean sanctum with a conspiratorial air. And within, hidden behind the unnecessary bunk bed lest the proctor should happen to manifest himself, was the forbidden female form of Annabelle. She came of a fairly large family, but her only elder was a sister, Lorie, so Sam had always been kind of a surrogate big brother to her. I don't clearly recall, but I believe they were painting something together on this particular occasion. What I do remember is being literally speechless when she stepped out—and that don't happen often. We became friends that night, and took the first uncertain step or two toward becoming more than that.

Now, I know what you're thinking. This abrupt deluge of emotional intensity in the immediate wake of an ugly break-up: how fair was I being to Anna by trying to give her a shattered heart? Well—I dunno. Beyond question she deserved better than me; but I *do* know my feelings for her weren't merely transference or "rebound" from Kara, because I still loved Annabelle for a long time. When we broke up, it was four and a half years before I dated again—but that's getting *way* ahead of the story.

One night we decided to go for a walk down the old train tracks near the college, only to find them fenced off. Fence-hopping being something of a specialty of mine, I ascended and perched at the top and attempted to essay an impromptu lesson on the rudiments of the climbing arts, until she said something on the order of, "Or I could just do this," and squeezed ethereally through the chained-up aperture. I could discern no rejoinder that would restore my coolness after such a thing, so I sort of went, "Oh, er, yes, or you could do that," and cleared my throat a few times in as manly a fashion as I could muster. That was Anna. Same night, we came to a quiet moment and I was racking my tiny brain for something romantic to say, when she turned and kissed me as if it were the most natural thing in the world—which I suppose, after all, it was.

The timing was unpropitious, mind you. We weren't together two weeks before the school year came to an end. I had no clear plans for my life; nothing could possibly have seemed less attractive to me than going back to Jotun at that point, and my academic career had met a ghoulish demise. Anna was spending the summer in Kansas with Lorie and her husband Ben, debating whether to head off to grad school or travel for awhile when September arrived. I still had some money saved up and had already promised to visit several TMC folk, so I determined to travel to that land of Superman's youth and see her again as soon as I could. I had a mournful premonition of how things were likely to end between us, given my general aimlessness and insolvency, but neither of us was ready to give up quite yet.

Sam and I, along with a few other guys, kicked off the summer with a road trip around New England, including a visit to Leah in Maine, where I was able to convince everyone that Papa John's pizza constituted a more exotic and glamorous dining experience than fresh lobster. (Leah wasn't too happy with me about that.) After that, I took a bus to go see Murtaugh in Iowa, where I got in a street-fight with a meth-head—my last fight until I got jumped by a drunk in Burlington in 2012, a guy who busted my brand new glasses. Most of the people I met there were meth- and/or pot-heads, I'm afraid, and to my Vermonter's eye, the place was hideously flat and corn-haunted, and also the Interstate had giant signs discouraging motorists from picking up hitch-hikers (which, thank God, a couple of motorists disregarded): in general, I didn't receive a very good impression of the state. There was, however, one major exception, which we'll come to shortly. Anyway, from Bancroft, Iowa, I made my way to Atchison, Kansas, where Annabelle waited.

Plato spins a myth in the *Symposium* to the effect that man and woman once were halves of a single happy creature, split in two by the gods lest in its self-sufficiency, this creature should grow too powerful to control. That was how I felt with her: part of a soul, complete. Ben and Lorie kindly quartered me while I was in town; and while Anna was working as a nanny for a local family during the day, I gladly served as temporary assistant nanny for the little ones, Peter and Joan. I have a penchant for horseplay and a deficient sense of personal dignity that seem to endear me to children for the most part, so we got along well. The rest of the time my lady and I spent together, mostly doing simple things like cooking or swinging or watching cartoons and just being with each other. On the Fourth of July we walked by the waters and watched the fireworks—and the next day, I made ready to depart.

My funds had run out and I needed work again; and besides, I had promises to keep (and miles to go before I'd sleep). From Kansas, my paths led to J.K.'s dwelling-place in Atlantic City. There are many tales I would tell of the Conclave—like the time we had to drag Luke away from a group of juniors with whom he was trying to start a brawl over a bottle of Ouzo, or the snowy evening when I knighted Smiles with a machete—but they're mostly tangential to our business here. The present point is that I wasn't moored to the 'clave as I'd been to the Kai; I visited the boys now and again, but never for long. I was adrift again, unstuck in time, a pilgrim lost in the bent cage of the world. But by the mysterious mercy which has ever hounded my steps, not only ineffable but inexorable, there continued to be dear friends nearby to steady me when I stumbled.

J.K. had an astounding ability to make things happen. We've all said, "Wouldn't it be fun to do such-and-such?" or, "Someday we ought to do so-and-so," only to forget all about it twenty minutes later. Well—my beloved friend and colleague lacks entirely that stoic center of the brain that's in charge of forgetting these things. Hence, when I was in A.C. in '04, he got wind that the Crossroads, a group that walks across the country every year to raise abortion awareness, was in Philly, and he single-handedly arranged for them to come speak at the local parish, Our Lady Star of the Sea; on the spur of the moment, he contacted a buddy and got them all free baseball tickets, too. When I was there in '09, he randomly decided to have a Passover meal (his father was Jewish, though non-practicing), and over the course of a few days, put together a full-scale *seder,* complete with bitter herbs and a Hebrew-speaking friend reading from the Pentateuch. His parents, who took me in like a returning prodigal without knowing me from Adam, were wonderful people with no money or connections whatsoever; J.K.'s abilities derived solely from his natural friendliness and enthusiasm. As soon as I got to town, he pulled a string of some kind and got me a job at the Cybata Hotel, Casino & Spa.

I spent July in A.C., and turned twenty-seven on the twenty-sixth. At the Cybata, I was a phone operator, taking reservations and uttering our immutable Cybatic catch-phrase, "Enjoy your day." (My trainer Randy actually berated me once for not saying it to a distraught man who called to cancel his reservation because his father had just died. Heretic and apostate, I said "God bless," instead.) It remains the only sit-down job I've ever held, and I did rather enjoy my day there; but then one morning I suffered a sudden and total breakdown, walked out without notice, and went off to get horribly drunk. I can't even say precisely why—I guess the whole black year at TMC somehow caught up with me all at once. No matter where you go, there you are.

I wasn't done running yet, though. I'd been talking with Josh, and he wanted to take another road trip (he wasn't with me and Sam earlier); so I suggested a return to the land of Captain Kirk's youth to see the Grotto of the Redemption. This is a huge shrine to the Blessed Virgin, constructed by a single priest over the course of forty years, in the unassuming town of West Bend, Iowa. J.K. had also expressed an interest in seeing the Grotto, so we invited him along. Josh came down in old Seamus to collect us, and we went stabbing westward. As we set out, a supremely characteristic J.K. moment occurred (and I do love telling this story). My cousin and I had decided to pick up Anna and bring her to the Grotto as well; so when J.K. asked where we were going first, I said, "Little town called Atchison, you've probably never heard of it." And he said, "Atchison, *Kansas*? I know three people there!" And he whipped out his cell phone on the spot, made a call, and when we got to town we swung up to Benedictine College and there was a dude waiting to give us a tour of the local bars. J.K. had walked with the Crossroads in high school, and kept in touch with every mother's son he met between the seas.

So the four of us set sail through the never-ending fields of golden corn, and spent a blue August afternoon wandering the giant shrine outside Sts. Peter and Paul Church. Walls, a courtyard, stairways, turrets—all built from pebbles and scraps of coral, over decades of devotion. When I asked my Anna what she thought of it, all she said was, "Being is good." It was no small admission for her. As you might expect from someone who felt so deeply about everything, she was often profoundly unhappy, a waifish doppelganger to my own rage and despair, and there wasn't much I could do on those days except to hold her as tightly as I could.

But it wasn't tight enough, and she slipped away from me. A couple of days later, back in Atchison, she slashed the thread of that dangling escrima stick of Damocles and went from being my Anna back to being just Anna again. I've never blamed her; I was a grown man (chronologically, anyway) with no job, prospects, education, or ambition, and besides, I was going back east indefinitely and she'd decided she was going off to Belgium—so the whole thing simply wasn't meant to be. Also, she didn't exactly say this, but we were growing awfully close, and I think maybe she was wary of letting herself fall in love, having been badly hurt before. And because I too had been hurt, I didn't fight to keep her.

In any case, I turned and headed for the east coast with the brothers of my heart, still not quite realizing how badly I'd been damaged since I flew from the eyrie of the Kai. Josh and I dropped J.K. in Atlantic City and went back "home," in the sense of going to Vermont. Feeling the need of some solitude, I got him to leave me at the Shrine of St. Anne on Isle La Motte, hard by the Canadian border. Now, I've never had a vision or witnessed anything a secularist would acknowledge as a miracle, but the Lord's always been pretty good about sending me dramatic weather. No sooner did I get to the little island fane than a hurricane swept through our land-locked state. And I was huddled in a doorway late one night, gazing out into the torrent, when I met my guardian angel. I've spent a very great deal of time alone during my lunatic peregrinations over the years, but although I often miss the people I love, I have never felt lonely—indeed, to speak more accurately, I have never felt alone. Tolkien says that just as the love between Father and Son is an actual Person, the Holy Spirit, so the love of God for each of us *is* our guardian angel, so powerful and unique that it becomes a separate, living soul. Lewis says that when we die and first lay eyes on that guard and guide whose loving presence has been with us since He formed us in the womb, our reaction will be not, "Who *are* you?" but rather, "So it was *you*, all this time!" I don't know what prompted me on that wild and windy night, but I found myself asking the darkness if there was an angel in it and, if so, by what name I should call him. And straightaway, not by a word but by an image I can't really explain, I was given to know that he was there, and had been and would be there, and that I could call him Toby. It was well for me, I think, that I began to know Toby when I did—because the bleakest part of this story was about to commence.

When I thumbed my way back to Josh's new place in Burlington, I learned that the federal government had contacted my parents in search of the loan money which, since I wasn't returning to TMC, I was now expected to repay. I talked to my mom in Alabama, and somehow—I don't even remember which of us first formulated the idea—the proposition arose that I should go back to 'Bama and stay with my folks until I had paid off the debt. And since I had no better plan, and was sick at the heart and fain to rest, I settled on that course. In early September I arrived back "home," in the sense of my father's house. And there my journey stopped for the next year and a half. Like a stricken bird curling up in her nest to die, I lost the world and forgot the call of road and sky; and if the soul weren't immortal, I suppose mine would have bled to death.

Kara. So much of my being had intertwined with hers—in pulling free, it was as if I'd spilled out all my pulsing organs in the dirt. My martial family was a thousand miles to the north, and scattered by the winds of grown-up life. The future was a black fog, my only certainty the fact that, once again, I'd failed and quit and run away. Annabelle, the glowing seraph in my dark night of the soul, was gone. And God, to Whom I'd just begun talking again, was utterly silent. I have never doubted

His existence—except one time—but during those crawling months in lightless places far from hope, I often doubted His love. There's no ground floor in Hell; even if you're only visiting, you can fall forever and ever.

I got a job stocking shelves at a dollar store, on the grave-yard shift. My heart kept beating, and the sun kept coming up. And as I corpse-walked through the desolation of my life, quiet grace and little mercies from the larger world settled on me like snowflakes, unnoticed but accumulating. Chris, eldest of the brothers Toner, now lived in Montgomery as well, and I got to know my sister Ruth and my nephews Patrick and William. Mom and I grew close again. Josh came to see me in May of '05, and I went to see Domingo in Colorado that October for a beer-fest (the wanderlust finally beginning to stir again). I had my first poems published, in a new magazine called *Dappled Things*. And one Sunday, when the Gospel reading was the Parable of the Prodigal Son, I found myself sobbing and embracing my dad for the first time in my life. We still can't be in the same room for ten minutes without pissing each other off—but something started to heal that day. Maybe if I make it to seventy and he to a hundred, we'll manage to become friends.

By the end of 2005, I had paid off my loans and stopped hemorrhaging from my wayward spirit. Even now I can't with certainty say what I learned during that time—"That night, that year of now done darkness I wretch lay wrestling with (my

God!) my God" ("Carrion Comfort," Hopkins). But perhaps my faith is a little tougher now. Old Fred, as everyone knows, observed that whatever doesn't kill you makes you stronger— and also, famously, "God is dead." Well, both statements are half true. God *was* dead, for three days. And yes, what doesn't kill you makes you stronger: but what *does* kill you, makes you stronger still. That's the blessing, as the far wiser Chesterton teaches us, of serving a God Who knows His way out of the grave.

The Kai
Re-forged

And now we're almost back to kicking ass.

But not quite. First I have to tell you about Santa Fe. In February of 2006, I packed my things—which is to say, some clothes, a few pens, and a notebook—and once more took a Greyhound west. Why Santa Fe? Dunno. I'd actually picked Albuquerque, solely because it's where Bugs Bunny always makes his wrong turns, but a friend of mine happened to mention how nice Santa Fe was, and I slightly altered my trajectory in consequence. I needed to go someplace new, I guess, and be alone again for awhile. I know, I know—it seems like I just did that a couple of pages ago, but remember that for me, a year and a half had gone by. In fact, that illustrates a forlorn motif in this silly symphony of mine: things that sound rapid and exciting in retrospect were often long and dull to live through, and moreover punctuated by interminable stretches of mental or physical discomfort. My friends have been telling me for years I should set forth an account of my idiotic misspent youth on paper, but I can hardly convey the full sense of weary, dragging *time* that pervades the space between memories—nor, if I could, would it be much fun to read about.

Anyway. Very nice town, Santa Fe; a desert and a mountaintop at the same time, cactus-flowers in snow. The night sky seems awfully close. I found a dry culvert right next to the library, and set up my sleeping bag and the plastic tarp that trapped in my body heat; there it stayed, along with all my meager possessions, for over forty days and nights, and no one ever tampered with it. I got a job at a nearby Sonic Drive-Thru (and it was there that I conceived the idea for my fabled drink, the Dr. Jones—four parts Dr. Pepper, one part eggnog, and a splash of maraschino cherry juice!), and passed a quiet Lent in what I came to call the City of the Stars. It's the only time in my life I've successfully fasted: I ate only two cans of fruit per day—except of course on Sundays, when I ate like a starving hog—and said the Rosary every night, and that was my whole life. I had and needed nothing except what He gave me. Every morning I bought a paper (which I never read) from a fellow homeless guy called Jerry, and every morning he said the same thing: "See you tomorrow, God willing." Ever since then, whenever I tell someone I'll see them later, I have always silently added that *Deo volente*. If we're honest, it should really be at the end of every sentence we utter about the future.

Some demons only leave us through prayer and fasting. When I came back to Burlington on Good Friday, I didn't *feel* any different on the surface. But very, very often, the Holy Spirit is most powerfully present at the times when we can't feel Him at all. Weeks—even months, I guess—went by as I gradually, glacially came to realize I'd been healed of the wounds I took in J-town. I was still adrift in the world and a child in many ways (and I'm kidding myself using the past tense here); but the great gift of waking up in the morning with a smile on my face had finally been returned to me. And then—ah, then—the Age of Ace began.

Ace Hardware! There I labored in both sun and rain for the next four years, with a brief caesura in 2009, and learned the making of many things. I should probably clarify that I'm almost comically "un-handy" and can barely tell at sight a lug-wrench from a hacksaw; snappin' spines and poetizin' all I be good at. Jake, my boss—and the best boss a working man could hope for—rarely left me in charge of customer assistance when it came to complex matters. I mixed paint, ran the register, carried stuff, and sometimes (aw yeah) drove the forklift. I called the forklift Bob, and it was the high point of my week to drive old Bob, except on those frequent occasions when he was malfunctioning; then there was such strife and hatred between us as could lay waste to an empire. Accursed Bob. No! I don't mean it, Bob, you're the only forklift in the world for me. *Damn you!*

Okay, but seriously. Josh was living with our friend Juan and another of our Jotun kith by the name of Max. It so happened that right as I was arriving in B-town, Juan's lady Gabriella was looking for a roommate; so we got ourselves a place a mile or two up the road from my cousin and literally across the street from Ace. Ella had a lovely newborn daughter called Kendra, and, during the year we lived together, I got to watch that unbelievably tiny repository of human and Heavenly history learn to crawl and walk and say "Mommy" and "Joshee" and "Jamey." That was a good year. I haven't seen my dear friend Ella for awhile, but I know she'd want me to relate the anecdote of the time she accidentally combined bleach and ammonia while cleaning the toilet. You know not to do that, right? Because it makes poison gas? Ella didn't! I stood there and watched her do it, somehow unable to believe it was happening; and a second later we were out in the hallway, choking and gasping for air. I don't even remember moving. It was pretty funny once we ventilated the place. (She's totally gonna kill me for telling that story.)

One of the blessings for which I am most grateful in our lives is that, during this time, Josh started teaching at St. Monica's K-8 in the next town over. It was there that he began to be among profoundly Christian people for the first time—and, in particular, it was there that he met Fr. Montfort, who is the holiest person I have ever known. I truly hope that some things I've said or done over the years may have been small vessels of grace for Josh as he made his way home; but it was at St. Monica that he tumbled into the cataract at last. By 2007 he was in RCIA, and that Easter he was received into the Church. But I'm getting ahead of the story again. Let's talk karate.

You see, Josh had obtained permission for the two of us to offer a children's self-defense class for the St. Monica kids when the new school year opened in September of '06. As the preceding year ('05–'06) came to an end in June, I was settling into my new place and my new job, and things were calm and stable for the first time in God knows how long; and Josh had a good chunk of the next three months off. Neither of us had trained seriously since camp of '03, and we wanted to be in fighting form when September rolled around—so we decided to spend the summer hammering ourselves back into shape. My buddy Murtaugh from TMC came to visit about this time and ending up crashing with me and G. for over a month, so Josh and I dragged him along to our ghastly sessions and taught him things about pressure and pain that no one with a functioning sense of empathy wants to know. A lot of what we did was simple conditioning; push-ups and wind sprints and so forth, obviously, but also a new invention we decided to call "power basics." Basics are the elementary punches and kicks with which every class commences, both as a warm-up and to keep the movements engraved on the muscle memory; the distinction was that in power basics, we did each technique (nineteen hand-strikes and seven kicks) absolutely as hard as we could for the duration of an entire song on the training CD we mixed for the purpose. Over an hour of torment! *Goooood times*. After that, grappling. I believe I've mentioned how thoroughly I enjoy that particular discipline; perhaps it's only fair to record additionally that Murtaugh did *not* share my enjoyment, but he struggled through it like a man.

It was also during that summer that I got to know that crazy, sacred sister of mine, my little bean, Miranda, Josh's love. They'd been dating since '05, and poor Miranda had been hearing stories about me for months. We'd met before, of course, in '02—but by this time she was so nervous about securing my good opinion that the first long phase of our friendship was marked by her incessant habit of bringing me baked goods almost every single time I saw her. I didn't object to receiving baked goods, mind you; but it did take me awhile to convince her that I was already inclined to think well of her since she made my cousin happy. Anyway, it's impossible not to love Miranda. She's like a grown-up Lucy from Narnia stirred together with Tigger from Winnie-the-Pooh. I was already fairly cheerful about the idea of having her as a cousin-in-law; but she and Josh had a long road ahead of them, and there was still a certain Test for her to pass.

As I say, we'd been out of practice most of the last three years, and our kindred in the Kai had fared much the same. Me and Josh leaving was part of the reason. Also, Sensei and Lissa had been having compatibility problems, and had separated and gotten back together a couple of times; ultimately, to our sorrow, Lissa asked him for a divorce. I've heard both sides of the thing, and this is hardly the place to give a judgment even if it were my right to do so—but Lissa ended up marrying old Groo, the JSC security guard, and I have to say this for Sensei: he could have poured that man over his Corn Flakes if he'd chosen to, but he never raised a hand in violence. D.J., Susannah, Tim, Ned, Riggs. . . most of us moved away after '03, some only as far as Essex or Burlington, some as far as California. Our fellowship was broken.

But with the coming of September and the inauguration of the school gym as our new dojo, something began to stir in the ashes. Our first student was a sixth grader by the name of Bryan, a shy, good-natured kid whom we were determined to twist into a maniacal killing machine. Well, that's what *I* wanted to do; Josh really just wanted to give him some self-confidence and a little basic conflict resolution know-how. And our boy learned those lessons well enough to give a bitter old man like myself hope for the rising generation. Within a few months, as the group expanded, Bry was leading basics at the start of every class—and within three years, he became the Kai's first junior *sho-dan*. When he and Violet, our second student, got their yellow belts, Sensei came up to B-town to meet them and bestow the patriarchal blessing, so to speak; and that helped to re-kindle the sunken blaze of our martial brotherhood. (And sisterhood.) We soon learned that Arnold and Renee had been training on their own back in Jotun, and it wasn't too long before Sensei and T. started bringing them up to meet our kids and link the spreading branches of the Kai.

Several adults—including the elderly organist from St. Monica's Church next door—came and went during the next couple of years, along with over a dozen kids ranging from second grade to eighth. Most notably, Bryan's mom Debbie ended up joining us, and she is still one of our best students. In 2007, his younger siblings—the twins Karen and Coleman, then in fifth grade—came on board as well, both of them characterized by a level of energy that I'm convinced could power a small city if one could somehow keep them pointed in a consistent direction for any length of time (a perpetual challenge with the twins). Karen's rambunctiousness often manifested itself in the form of bizarre and random questions; I remember her asking Josh once why he was bald ("Because I've got no hair"), and she was constantly asking me why my socks didn't match ("Huh? Oh—because—er—I—because—do your push-ups, urchin!"). Coleman, for his part, once saw me run up the wall and hang from the basketball hoop, and he made it his goal in life to do the same, despite a critical height differential. Every week as we were stretching before class, he would take a running start from the far side of the floor, sprint the length of the gym, and splatter himself against the crash mats on the wall like a tiny blond Wile E. Coyote—and never lose his smile. Watching those super-sonic bundles of hyperactivity tear around our makeshift dojo, I've always regarding Deb with admiration, sympathy, and maybe just a little bit of envy. This book is dedicated to a man called Earl, a great teacher and a great friend; but, if I'm allowed to double up like this, I'd also like to dedicate it to those four.

In July of '09 (to jump ahead for a moment), we re-convened at the old dairy farm and held our first black belt camp in six long and difficult years. As ever in days of old, we trained like madmen through the grueling days and nights, tuning ourselves up to concert pitch, until the sun went down and the final dusk arrived. Then, as ever, we built our giant fire. Bryan had just graduated from St. Monica and was heading off to high school—and he would be arriving there as one of *us*. That year, Arnold too achieved his black belt at last. He and Bry stood side by side, and the Tap-Out began. D.J. was gone; Dean-O, a new *kyu*, handled the drums. Craig and Lissa weren't with us that year either, so once again the honor fell to the four of us, the core of us: me, Josh, T., and the man himself, our Sensei. At the height of the Ceremony, Josh and I peeled off and got behind Arnold, and Sensei body-checked him like a freight train. We tried to catch that hurtling colossus, but you might as well stare down an avalanche with a snow-blower. Once Josh extricated himself from the flailing heap of *sho-dan* we three had become, he plunged across the circle, tackled our Bry, and bore him away like a sack of grain. Then T. and I dragged Arnold away from the fire and into the forest and off to the moonlit waters of initiation. And so, after what seemed whole ages of the earth, the Kai brought forth new black belts once again.

In our strange inconclusive showdown more than a decade earlier, Biloxi Bob had called me a *ronin*—a masterless warrior, outcast and directionless, fighting only for himself—and at the time, it was absolutely true. But no longer. Ask me who I am and I'll say I'm a son of the Church: I *try* to keep that foremost, and may God forgive my endless failures. *Domine, non sum dignus.* But whatever worth I have—whatever strength, wisdom, or virtue I've been granted—it's because of the martial arts that I know what to do with it. It was the Kai that taught me how to be a part of something, how to belong. And it's because of that lesson that I'm (slowly, slowly) coming to accept my place, not as a lone epic hero, but as a member of the team, the family, the Mystical Body of Christ.

On the Road Again

A few noteworthy things happened in 2007, although mostly not to me. In the first week of January, Domingo got married to a very cool chick called Sarah, whom I'd met a couple of years earlier in Colorado, and I flew out to Vegas for a laid-back wedding at Caesar's Palace. There, thanks to my friend's magnanimity and a non-refundable pre-paid bar tab, I got to have a few glasses of Cristal; and, speaking as one whose connoisseurship rarely extends beyond Carlo Rossi and Boone's Farm, I must say that the stuff is well worth a fortnight's salary (on very special occasions). In February, our little B-town circle performed a Chinese fire drill of domiciles: Juan moved in with Ella, taking my place; Max emigrated to Bennington in southern Vermont; and Josh and I got a new place, only a little farther away from Ace, which we dubbed the Kilburn High after a Flogging Molly song. About that time, he enrolled in RCIA, with me as his nominal sponsor, though I'm afraid I didn't do much. Also that year, Miranda chose to receive the Sacrament of Baptism, and asked me to be her Godfather, which was quite an honor, though again I didn't really do anything remarkable. And, lessee, in July, I turned thirty. Probably at least a minor miracle that I've somehow managed to survive this long despite all the absurd things I've done in the last fifteen years—heck, I've never even broken a bone—but most of the credit for that must be imputed to Providence, Toby, and all the people who love me. Other than these incidents, I basically got up each day, went to work, and came home.

I am truly proud of only two accomplishments thus far in my floundering, rudderless existence. One of them, and I don't imagine this will surprise anyone, is the earning of my black belt. But the other one will probably sound rather mundane, not to say anticlimactic. You see, when Josh and I signed our lease at the Kilburn, I promised my cousin I'd stick around for two full years before I went wandering off again. Now, that may be an almost overwhelmingly standard and non-extraordinary arrangement between American adults who take it as a given that sleeping under a ceiling is more normal than sleeping under a bridge or a bush. But I'm homeless—I was so born, and I expect I'll so die—and while I'm often homeless *indoors*, I still don't feel at home in any meaningful sense, wherever I alight. Never have. All Christians know that this indistinct middle earth, poised between Perdition and Paradise, is only a way station; but for whatever ineluctable reason, it's been ordained that I should experience it as a continuous emotional reality. Two years in one spot—ye gods, I felt like a rat in a coffee can.

'07 was the longest year I've ever lived through. Externally, it was a great year—I was living in a nice apartment with my best friend, working full-time with wonderful people (the Ace crew went an awfully long way toward keeping me sane), well-fed and in perfect health, with no malaise to speak of but the cold iron trap of the quotidian, the slow creeping of the days and hours and minutes, the ticking ennui of a peered-at clock. And believe me, I'm aware of how overwrought that sounds, and of how cheerfully the emaciated denizens of, say, Port-au-Prince or Calcutta would have swapped problems with me; I was dimly aware of that even at the time, but it didn't alter the way I felt. It wasn't as if I had anywhere else to go, particularly. It was just knowing that I *couldn't*. Nor did it help that I was too wrapped up in my various broodings to think of going out to volunteer at the Salvation Army or take an Irish dancing class or, you know, buy a cape and fight crime: anything to drag me out of myself. Yet I'm not sure—it may have been better so. With no distractions or assistance whatsoever, I was compelled to suck it up and stick it out solely because I'd given my cousin my word. It was a test I'd failed before. By the time 2008 rolled around, I was finally measuring time no longer in months but in years. (Hence my incessant habit of rattling off '05s and '98s and what have you like a World War I vet. It's how I keep track of my wayfaring ways.)

'08 was a lot better. For some reason, I suddenly started writing again—and I discovered that, though I say it who shouldn't, I'd improved enormously and, as it were, spontaneously since my ordeal at TMC. I actually remember hearing the old cliché as a kid, that one must suffer to become an artist, and wondering what on earth it meant and whether it was bosh; but I don't know, there seems to be something in it after all. Solzhenitsyn once said something to the effect that he was appalled to think how shallow his writing would have been if he'd never endured the Soviet persecution. (And Walker Percy once said that American writers secretly envy Solzhenitsyn for his time in the gulag.) Comfortable in the Kilburn Archipelago, I beguiled the hours with writing and work and teaching and prayer, and eventually 2009 came gliding up the time-stream.

'09 started well. I'd made it. I'd kept my word. That's my other big accomplishment, and I know it don't sound like much. Even to myself at this current vantage—and it's only been a couple of years—the notion of staying in one place for a comparable duration in the future no longer sounds especially daunting; but, I presume, that's precisely because I've now done it once already: broken the seal, if you will. I gave Jake, my boss, notice at the year's dawn that I'd be taking off in March when my lease expired, and sailed blithely through the next two months. My plan was to head down the east coast visiting friends from TMC. But something singular occurred as February drew to a close.

As you may surmise, I was flying pretty high at this particular juncture. I felt as if I'd gone up a level, so to speak, and the road lay open before me. "All the lights are turning green," as Miranda put it. In this elevated mood, as I was going through a few belongings that I planned on leaving behind in Josh's keeping, I came across a letter I'd written five years earlier. It was addressed to myself ten years later—that is, to whomever I'll be in 2014—and sealed up in a common envelope along with the Miraculous Medal I got from Kateri back in New Hampshire. I have no recollection of the letter's contents—find out in another couple years, I guess—but I recall putting her medal in the envelope because it's one of only two physical objects I treasure on earth. (The other's a rosary that Sam hand-made for me in Peru. It's around my neck as I write this.) I've always had a strange relationship with Kateri. She's a nurse and a dancer and a Tolkien lover, and she's mischievous and sweet as a wood sprite, but also tough enough that she once hiked for miles with a broken ankle in Ireland looking for a doctor, and her smile is so, so beautiful. We were friends at TMC, saw each other every day, and had a million things in common, but somehow we could never seem to talk to each other. There was a good deal of, "Hi." "Hi!" "Sooooo—how's stuff?" "Pretty good." "Good!" And shuffling of feet and awkward scratching of the back of one's head. And I have no idea why. I love her, she's dear as the stars to me, but there's a click somewhere that we've never quite managed to clack.

Well, I came across this letter and I found myself thinking about her, and I realized I hadn't seen her in years and I missed her. Then, before I had time to think about it, I found myself writing her an email of the self-declaratory sort, vowing to change the world for her and really, really meaning it. I'd barely heard from her since the Conclave graduated; for all I knew, she was days away from takin' a hubby or taking the veil. But a few hours later, she wrote me back, and the gist of it—not wishing to violate the confidences of a lady or anything—was that she was unattached and thought well of me, and that I ought to come visit her in Massachusetts so we could try actually getting to know each other a bit. Naturally, this made me tremendously happy. And, because the Enemy knows a fool when he sees one, my happiness was almost immediately toppled into hubris—and that's when the event occurred.

This gigantic sense of victory behind me—this dawn-lit vista of freedom and promise ahead—all this I had carved out for myself, I thought, ignoring the countless days I couldn't put one foot before another and had to be half-dragged, half-carried along by grace—with my mind and my strength, all this was mine for the seizing, and who needed God anyway? Maybe there was no God in the first place. It came into my head, and instantly everything disintegrated. For a brief moment, for the one and only time in my life (thank God), I stumbled into the atheist's universe and found it indistinguishable from Hell. There's nothing—*nothing*. No transcendence, no meaning, no hope; nothing bigger than ourselves, a wilderness of mirrors, a sparrow flying through a lighted feasting-hall by night, out of darkness and back to darkness; skulls, maggots, empty places between stars, and nothing waiting for us at the end of it all: absolutely nothing. Why not suicide, indeed? Why not *murder*, if there is no immortality?—just for the fun of the thing. I had a pretty vivid image of myself covered in blood—don't know whose—and then I was sobbing on the floor and begging God to be there, to be real. Abba, Father, Daddy—please don't leave us alone.

That was the worst moment of my life. Accidentally discharging my rifle at Fort Benning, getting stripped of my black belt, finding Kara in bed with a stranger—none of those moments even compare. I knew Mother Theresa had said that in times of doubt we can *will* ourselves to have faith, so I spent the next few hours muttering, "I believe. I believe. I believe." Soon enough the doubting passed; and I was vastly the better for that brief doubt because, Holy Mother of God, did it smash the arrogance out of me. At least for the time being. Pride is a difficult weed to cut, and the roots go bedrock-deep.

Once I pulled myself together, I chartered a bus and broke south. First I went to D.C. to visit Sam, and he showed me the sights: the Smithsonian, the Monument, the Vietnam Wall. Then, while my patriotic fervor was at its height, I returned to Atlantic City to follow J.K. on the campaign trail for mayor. Yes: most of the nomenclature in this account has been tweaked to protect the innocent (although I use my mom and dad's real names, which are Mom and Dad), but my most excellent friend J.K. is none other than the honorable Jesse O'Leary Kurtz, the 2009 Republican A.C. mayoral candidate. He lost out that year, alas, to Langford the incumbent; but I offer his name in case any good citizen of New Jersey should chance to see it on a ballot in the future. The man's not only a genius at what he does, but a truly generous and kind-hearted human being—and wouldn't it be interesting to have an honest politician in office, just for a change of pace?

In late April I made it back to Massachusetts and re-united with Kateri. For one day, the wall of whatever was down between us, and we spent it going to lakes and parks and libraries and bowling alleys and climbing on trees and towers and tanks and getting rained on and walking down a bridge full of flowers and talking about everything in the world. It was one of my best days ever, and a welcome counter-weight to that dreadful day only a few weeks before. By May—mulching season at Ace and our busiest month—I had drifted on back to Vermont and gotten my old job again. I slept in the greenhouse out back until November and then rented a room (a basement, actually) for the winter from my co-worker Wayne at his house, which I inevitably came to dub Stately Wayne Manor. Kateri and I dated long-distance for over a year but ultimately decided we were meant to be friends, not lovers—and when we broke up, I went wandering off yet again.

But now I fear the tale has run overlong. Josh became principal of St. Monica's, one of the youngest principals in Vermont, and he and Miranda (who nailed the Returning Cousin Test with flying colors) are now married, God bless them, after a beautiful Mass by Fr. Montfort, who is now Monsignor Montfort. Renee earned her black belt in 2010 and is currently engaged to T., a betrothal which in all likelihood will continue unconsummated for decades to come (sometimes our boy procrastinates a bit). Deb and Coleman got their black belts in 2012, along with T.'s sister Jenna. (I tapped Coleman out myself, and hoooo dawgy, did I drill that kid!) Sensei's working security at JSC, where the students are now quite exceptionally secure, and seeing a very nice girl called Cheryl. The Kai goes on. As for me: I've made some new friends and had some peculiar adventures; but like the song says, I still haven't found what I'm looking for. I've been on the road again, lo these many months, and I begin to feel—at long, long, long, long last—that I should make something worthwhile, something worthy, out of all the endless mercies I've been given. And I don't know how to make anything else, so I've made this book. I don't know how much real wisdom it contains, but perhaps if you're feeling aimless in your life, you can take some solace in reflecting, "Well, at least I'm not that Toner guy." Still—for all of us who wander in this vale of tears below, there's another song that tells a higher truth: "Through many dangers, toils, and snares I have already come; 'tis grace has brought me safe this far, and grace will bring me home."

Only Thyself

I once met a guy who claimed to be a Druid, and he told me he could hit me from across the room with a technique he called the Celtic Wave Attack. When I expressed a reasonable skepticism toward this alleged ability, he demonstrated by waving from across the room to his buddy, who was standing next to me. His buddy punched me. A silly trick, you may well say, but it gave me the chance to re-secure an important truth which had fallen into pagan hands. (Justin Martyr: if it's true, it's Christian.) That truth is—to a wise warrior, pride is at best an irrelevancy and, at worst, the prelude to a fall. No matter how smart you may be, if you're fighting for ego, you'll behave stupidly and leave yourself vulnerable. Those guys already knew they were tough; they had nothing to prove to themselves. Why risk losing a tooth to a vain and foolish boy when they had the advantage of numbers? If Beowulf had heeded his retainers and not arrogantly fought the Fire-drake one on one, his people might not have lost their king.

The Chinese invented kung-fu (the word means simply, "skill"); they also invented gunpowder, which superseded it. In the 1970s, movie-going Americans half-believed that kung-fu could give a man magical invincibility—then in the '80s it was karate, in the '90s jujitsu, and in the double-aughts this new-fangled "Mixed Martial Arts" that everyone in the UFC is practicing all of a sudden. But as anybody with a working hand-gun will cheerfully explain, none of these skills can make someone invincible or anywhere close to invincible. Just as every storyteller knows that there are essentially only ten plots in all of literature (search for God, search for love, search for vengeance, etc.), so every martial artist ought to realize that there has been no fundamental change in the potentialities of the human form since Adam counted his limbs and invented the number four. If we could travel back to ancient Athens and wrestle in the first Olympics, we wouldn't have many tricks that the old Greeks didn't already know. (Fun fact: Plato's real name was Aristocles. "Plato" was a nickname that meant "broad shoulders.") And although our martial athletes today wear a very tiny bit more clothing than the Olympians of antiquity, little else has really changed. The UFC isn't fighting. It's a *sport*. And I'm sure that for whatever it's worth, even the smallest UFC competitor could kick the living daylights out of me in a fair fight: which is why, if anything more important than my ego were at stake, I would never fight him fairly. Not when the march of science has put so many alternatives to bare-handed combat at my disposal.

So! What is the point of this apparently belligerent diatribe? Actually just the opposite of what it appears. I don't wish to discuss who can beat up whom (in a technocratic society, how much does it honestly matter?)—still less, God knows, to denigrate the arts as a whole. I merely wish to place them in their proper context. In the Middle Ages, aspiring philosophers were required to study law, not so they could moonlight as litigators, but because the discipline of jurisprudence taught them to think *logically*. In the same way, our Special Forces operatives are taught advanced martial arts, not in the expectation of disabling enemy missiles with jump kicks, but to help inculcate mental and physical toughness. However—as ordinary Christian folk going about our day-to-day lives, how in the world can you and I draw spiritual benefits from knowing exactly where to poke a dude to seal off his trachea?

As I conceded earlier, I lack the learning to discuss the ethics of combat in universal terms; for that, you must go to my old man. Try his *Morals Under the Gun*, from the University of Kentucky Press, for a scholarly treatment of the subject. All I have to offer are three insights, or maybe just notions, based on my own highly peculiar and idiosyncratic experiences, and I hope they may be of some small value. The first is this. The arts enabled me to grasp as a concrete, rather than sensing as an abstract, that although there are perhaps as many roads to truth as there are human souls, there is ultimately but a single truth. I believe in principle that each man finds his own destiny; I know in practice that every martial artist makes his own martial art, from all he's learned and then rejected, from all he's jury-rigged or improvised to fit his own environment and body type, from all he's picked up from movies or friends in other schools or his own imagination, and most of all from what he's grate-fully accepted from his masters and their masters before them. *But*—the individuality of the method does not mean that the goal is subjective. Rather the reverse: it's precisely because the goal is fixed and immutable that we can confidently approach it from any direction. Chesterton says no two people are less alike than two saints, because they've fully actualized the unique potential assigned to each of them by God. You might say they learned to glow in their own particular color; whereas when we first begin to learn, we're all white belts, containing a mix of every color possible. *And we find our own specific path by submitting to a general discipline.* Which (by a mighty cosmic coincidence) leads neatly to my second notion.

St. Augustine, setting forth what is probably the ballsiest theological maxim in all of Christendom, said simply, "Love God and do what you will." Second part's easy. Sure I love God, now bring on the booze! Problem is, true love for God has to manifest as love for Christ in our neighbors: "Whatsoever you do to the least of My people, that you do unto Me" (Matthew

25:40). And true love for our neighbors has to manifest as self-sacrifice, because that is how God's love operates—it's how His love for us manifested as Jesus—and we cannot love truly by our own power. We have to borrow His love to love with, and that means loving the way He does, which is often exciting but never easy. Why is it so hard? Because we're *fallen*. We can't trust ourselves to be virtuous by instinct. It's why we need clothes. It's also (and yes, we are still talking about martial arts here) why we need *rules*. We cannot figure everything out for ourselves. We of the Kai have encountered many legitimately tough guys over the years who have "learned" to grapple by watching the UFC and screwing around with their buddies, and so far we've beaten all of them. Whatever little tricks they've thought up on their own, whole generations of warriors have already systemized a dozen ways to counter them, and we learned it all the only way you learn anything—by doing it over and over again until it's ingrained. Yes, the ultimate goal is to transcend the rules, to internalize the spirit behind the letter so thoroughly that you no longer need to worry about observing the rituals and formulae. But how do you do that? By observing the rituals and formulae.

I once read a work called *The Book of Five Rings* by the famous samurai Miyamoto Musashi, undefeated in over sixty death-matches. He gives a torrent of what is no doubt useful advice about sword-fighting; but, not being a sword-fighter, I failed to retain any of it (except that apparently you can kill a guy if you ram your shoulder into his chest hard enough). What I do remember is that nearly every paragraph concluded with, "You must train diligently in this," or "You must study this well." Being charitable to others isn't a decision, it's a process. We have to train diligently in it. Loving God doesn't just mean sticking our heads into a church on Sunday morning. Traveling toward holiness means acting through and with and in Him at every moment of the day. Sounds daunting, but it's only a matter of practice. The master shows his art in every movement: over time, it becomes a habit that permeates our lives. You'll often hear people say they believe in "spirituality" but not organized religion, which ranks right up there with "Jesus wasn't God but a great human teacher" at the top of the "haven't thought through what I'm saying" scale. It sounds marvelously broad-minded on the surface; the problem is, there's nothing under-neath. No depth, no bones. It's a philosophy for amoebae. If you're building a ziggurat, you can't start at the apex; we reach the upper spheres of perfect freedom *after* we've been taught to desire what we ought to desire. "Ah," one might object, "but the voice of the Lord in my heart. . ."—is, let us admit, pretty easy to hear saying whatever we want it to say unless our fellow men check us from time to time. In much the same way, I was industriously cementing myself into punching habits that were comfortable, easy, and utterly wrong until Sensei corrected my form. And he did that by forcing me to obey the established rules. I'm afraid I still punch a good deal better than I pray, and

I don't yet trust myself to follow Augustine's dictum on my own—but I hope and believe that if I keep on trying, my soul will grow stronger in time. Right now I'm doing push-ups with my knees on the ground, so to speak. And when you're dealing with the Almighty, being on your knees is never a bad idea.

Which brings us to my third and final notion. There's an old debate over the function of bodily posture in prayer and devotion: do we really have to kneel to talk to God? Do we have to go to a physical building on the Sabbath to be gathered in His name? Pretty clearly, the answer is "not always." We can talk to God all the time, at work or in bed or while reading or running or watching TV. But the answer's also "yes, often." We're not pure spirits. That's the whole *point* of us. We're the kids that got bodies like the beasts and animae like the angels. Best of both worlds—at least, until we screwed it up in Eden and the worlds of matter and spirit came unglued. But the fact remains: what we do with our bodies affects our everlasting souls. If our minds seek reverence, what could be more sensible than to begin by adopting a reverent posture? Besides, let's bear in mind that the nexus and crux of the whole salvific history of the universe occurred when the Word became flesh. Jesus was constantly touching people and breathing on them and rubbing, for Pete's sake, mud and spit in their eyes by way of healing their afflictions; and the supernatural grace of the Sacraments comes to us through the medium of plain corporal things like oil and water and wine. In our physical selves, the

Eternal is enacted through the temporal, and all is hallowed. Our flesh is sacred, and will rise again.

And what exactly does all this have to do with martial arts? Okay—I'll admit that at this point, my thinking gets a little mystical. ("I think we passed mystical about three exits back, Toner." Yeah, yeah, just bear with me here.) One summer when we were in high school, Josh was spending a couple of weeks at Gram and Grampy's farm (I was down in 'Bama at the time) and was given the task of mowing the giant lawn. It was a task he loved, since it involved piloting Grampy's huge new riding mower, and he'd just gotten his license and thought he was the best driver since Elwood Blues. On a fine sunny afternoon beneath a bright blue sky, he drove that monster up a steep hill out behind the house and it flipped right over on top of himself. He's still got a grim-looking scar on his leg where the gearstick tore him open so wide you could see the naked muscles coiling over bone. Now, Grampy was a tough enough guy, like everyone in his generation—he was a Seabee in the War in the Pacific—but only a man, and well into his seventies by this time. But when his grandson rolled that mower and was pinned square underneath it, screaming in terror and pain, he came running up the hill and he lifted the whole thing off with his bare hands. Closest thing to an out-and-out miracle yet vouchsafed to our family.

So—was it supernatural what happened that day? Did Josh's guardian angel give a hand with the lifting? Or was it simply the natural order as it was originally intended to be, re-asserting itself for a moment? The natural world, after all, exists solely because it is pervaded and sustained at every instant by that which lies beyond it. Many people have speculated that Jesus' miracles were performed not through His divine nature but through His perfected human nature. C.S. Lewis even wondered if we should be ashamed of not performing miracles. After the Second Coming and the Resurrection of the Dead, we'll all be walking around (and ah, God, I hope also *flying*) in glorified bodies capable of all manner of incredible things: we shall be like Him, for we shall see Him as He is (1 John 3:2). But I often wonder—mightn't that potential already lie within us, untapped? That's not ultimately the point, of course; one doesn't go to church thinking, "A few more decades of this and I'll get to dodge bullets!" Union with the Father through Christ is the point. But still—seek ye first the Kingdom, and all these things shall be added unto you (Matthew 6:33). Right?

I dunno, guys. I guess it's taken me this whole inane book to admit that in studying the arts, I'm always secretly hoping to figure out how to punch through a tank someday. What then becomes of my initial thesis, "Do all to the glory of God"? Well—it's a goal. I ain't there yet, but at least I can see where I'm trying to get to. Most of what I do is still motivated by selfishness. But I'm trying, Lord. I'm trying.

When St. Thomas Aquinas wrote his treatise on the Eucharist, the carven Christ in his chapel stepped down from the great crucifix and said, "Thomas, thou hast written well concerning this doctrine of My Body." Then He offered Thomas a gift, any gift of his choice, from all the mysteries of Creation by the hands of Omnipotence Incarnate. And Thomas said, "I will have Thyself. *Only* Thyself." He chose well, for Jesus is joy and in Him are all joys contained; but even the great philosopher and saint had to live out his earthly time before going home to the full granting of that gift. We visit the mountaintop to be transfigured, but we're not meant to *stay* there: we're meant to go back down and spread the good news however each of us can. Martial arts may not be the most promising way, but it's all I've got to offer, so I trust God to make use of me in His own ineffable fashion. I certainly expect no reward—I'll be happy enough merely to be spared my just punishments—but if He ever offers me a choice of gifts, I truly hope I'll have the grace and sense to answer as Thomas did. Give me Thyself, O Lord. Only Thyself.

Amen.

Conclusion: 2012

There's an old Chinese curse: "May you live in interesting times." It's a conjuration that can go several levels deep, depending on how you look at it; but as you've no doubt noticed by now, I'm fond of examining the double-edged sagacity of the virtuous pagans in the light of their Christian descendants. Chesterton puts it this way: "An inconvenience is only an adventure wrongly considered. An adventure is only an inconvenience rightly considered." Interesting times certainly *can* be a curse, but they needn't be. The trick is keeping in mind that life is a quest. I've been both blessed and blighted by the many strange adventures I've been given over the years, and I feel they've trained me well for the unknown tasks awaiting me now. The past, as they say, is prologue.

As I emerge from the long, echoing corridor of half-remembered yesterdays and bring this chaotic volume to a close, I'm humbled by the sheer magnitude of my debts. If I tried to thank everyone I ought to, this conclusion would be only the preface to a much larger book; but I'm grateful to all who have shared the road with me and helped me with my burdens, real or imagined. I hope after all the stupid things I've done, I may yet do something to justify your faith in me.

I'm thirty-five now, and I still don't know where the hell I'm going. But in writing this account, I've come to perceive and accept that I don't always need to know. I just need to trust. "Let it be done to me according to Thy word." My part, at least for now, is simply to keep putting one foot in front of the other and trying to offer all the little things I do to the glory of the Triune God. All things work to the good for those who love Him.

So pray for me, brothers and sisters, and may the Light shine on your path. Or rather, *our* path, for we are the Church, and each of us is chosen for sainthood and a pivotal role in the Great Dance in which we all follow and lead, and even the Master washes the feet of His servants. Greater joy and strength and freedom than we in our broken state can yet imagine lie before us, and because Jesus is the Way, Heaven is already with us, even as we travel slowly toward it. The trials we've faced thus far have prepared us; the real quest commences today. The moment that we touch our eternal destiny is always *now*. Now—now we are ready to begin.

Coda: 2012–2022

You are the Chosen One.

And so am I. And so is that guy over there. That's what I've been trying so hard to learn all this time, never knowing what I was trying to learn. I remember walking down dark alleys at night in big cities, hoping for an "adventure," reasoning that if I was indeed special, then God wouldn't let anything happen to me—and if I wasn't, then my death would be no loss to the cosmos. It's taken me forty-five years to wrap my head around the simple and obvious fact that I've been chosen to do specific things that no one else in all of spacetime can do in precisely the way I can (like helping my wife to raise our beautiful daughters), and that the same is true of every human soul.

Not long after the final events recorded in The Kai, I had my last street fight. I was working nights as a janitor at a co-op in Burlington, Vermont; and one night, on my way to work, I was attacked by a rather large drunken fellow demanding a quarter. (A quarter! I would've given him a stupid quarter if he'd asked.) His first swing broke my glasses, and to this day I'm frustrated that I let such a wildly telegraphed loop connect with me. My only excuse is that, a few days earlier, Annabelle and I had broken up yet again after one last attempt at dating, and I was feeling rather low. I grabbed the guy, we went to the asphalt, and he put me in guard. Me! Everyone thinks they know bloody grappling now, thanks to MMA. I knelt there in his guard, debating wearily whether I even cared enough about this fight to pinch his femoral nerve and scramble into mount (don't ever do this during a friendly match, by the way), and ultimately deciding, "Eh—the heck with it." At that point, some college kids happened along and offered to call the cops; the guy turned me loose; I got up and went to work.

It didn't occur to me until later that this was precisely the scenario I'd daydreamed about so many times in the yore-times: assailed by desperados, forced to unleash my deadly skills, etc. When it finally happened, I just moped my way through the fight. God ain't subtle, folks: when you pray for something stupid, He'll answer it eventually; but He'll wait till you no longer want it, so you can realize how stupid you were.

I came to realize that I'd finally had enough of wandering and homelessness. Wintering in Steubenville, Ohio, was enough to freeze the chutzpah of hardier men than I; and besides, in the end, I'd achieved everything I set out to achieve. I used to think of myself as a Catholic, a writer, and a martial artist—in descending order of importance, of course—but the martial arts had taken the bulk of my unduly lengthy adolescence. I started studying my faith, learning about the Little Way and Teresian spirituality (Lisieux and Avila, respectively!); I got more serious about my writing. I moved into a house with some great guys, worked nights, and lived a quiet life.

And somewhere in the summer of 2012, I went to a karaoke bar and met Ellen. Again, most of the names in this book have been changed, but there's little point in changing the name that became Mrs. Toner. Many people don't believe in love at first sight, and they're wrong. My clearest memory of that night, apart from her nailing Norah Jones' "Lone Star," is of thinking, "Why couldn't I marry a girl like this? Exactly like this?" Happily, it transpired that I could.

I didn't declare myself at the time (possibly because Anna was there that night too), and it turned out that Ellie was moving to Alexandria, Virginia, the very next week. So, playing it perhaps just a teensy bit creepy, I found her blog ("Taking Back Our Brave New World") and read its entirety, thus very much confirming my infatuation with her brain as well as her voice and her smile, and then began emailing her. "I loved your article on thus and such! Here are my thoughts, whatcha think?" Being my perfect woman, she naturally turned out to share my love of epistolary camaraderie. We corresponded for over a year, my emails slowly growing less reticent about my feelings, until finally she suggested we meet in New York City to catch up. As it came about, she was quite unaware of how I felt (despite her friends telling her I was clearly a man in love), and she was a bit taken aback when I told her. But on Thanksgiving weekend of 2013, we officially started dating. Three weeks later, I told her I wanted to marry her.

It wasn't easy. In fact, it was far and away the hardest thing I'd done. I moved to Alexandria the next summer, found a house with more great guys, and got myself a job. Answering phones at a window installation place for ten dollars an hour. I had no driver's license, no college degree, no particular skillset. What I had was an ingrained pattern of shrugging off obligations when things got hard, and moving to a new town. But not this time. I gritted my teeth and held on, suffering some of the bleakest depression I'd faced to date, growing ever more convinced I'd never be able to marry my love. On Easter Monday of 2015, as I was visiting Mom and Dad on my way to Minnesota, where my sister-in-law Ruth had offered me a position as a nursing assistant once it became inescapably clear that I could no longer even make ends meet in Virginia, I got a call: our parish pastor needed a handyman. I hadn't even applied: our friend Morgan tossed out my name, and Fr. McGee said it sounded good. It had benefits, a future, and a marriageable wage. When I told Ellie that same day—her birthday, coincidentally—she wept because she knew we'd been saved.

We got married on December 12th of that year, the Feast Day of Our Lady of Guadalupe. It was a Latin Mass; Dad served as the deacon, and actually officiated the Marriage Sacrament for us. Ellie's little brother (as she endlessly delights in calling him), who at that time was still in the seminary, served on the altar. My friends came from every corner of the country to be with me, and we served Chipotle to over 200 guests before dancing the night away and being serenaded out the door with "Parting Glass" and "Non Nobis, Domine." That day remains probably the single best day of my life—so far.

We had our problems. (See Ellie's blog, "The Gate is Shut: Vaginismus in a Christian Marriage.") Once we overcame that, we had more problems: ever heard of hyperemesis gravidarum? I hadn't. Once she finally got pregnant—we found out on Father's Day 2017!—we learned that she suffers from a radical form of "morning" sickness that left her all but incapacitated for nine months. All to the good, though: it gave me plenty of time to grow in patience and nurturing. Our first girl was born in 2018, our second in 2019. We have a birthday for every season: Sonya's in winter, Ellie's in spring, mine in the summer, Rebecca's in fall.

Rebecca Eowyn, our youngest, bears my mother's name. Mom has Alzheimer's now, and is non-verbal. There's no telling where she and my dad will be by the time this book is published; but they feel ready for their hometown cemetery. Please pray for them, friends. It's been hardest on Dad, no doubt; but I miss my mama, whom I love so dearly. She hung on long enough to see me safely married, and to meet Sonya

Magdalena, her tenth grandchild (four from Chris and five from Pat), before she started what has been a rapid and sorrowful decline. We brought newborn Rebecca to her early in 2020, and hoped that she understood her name, but we don't really know. I'm grateful she and Ellie had time to come to love each other before mom began to lose her faculties.

We're in Massachusetts. We have a house, a garden, a dumb cat and a dumber dog, and a fluctuating number of chickens. I still work as a janitor, but it's first shift, and I get home to my girls by a quarter to four. I finally managed to publish a couple of novels in 2019 and 2020 (Whisper Music and The Shoreless Sea, if anyone's interested), although the combined royalties have not yet sufficed to buy me a twelve-pack of Miller, let alone hang up my mop for good.

Oh, speaking of Miller—I quit drinking, at long last. For my girls. On Monday evenings, I go to AA. I also, at Ellie's request, started seeing a therapist, who ultimately tested me for what used to be called Asperger's and found out that, hoo boy, do I ever have that! (Thankfully, these days, they call it Level One Autism, which sounds way cooler.) I was stunned, initially, by the diagnosis—like many in my "Shrinks're fer sissies" generation, I'd assumed autistic people were basically Rain Man—but exonerated as well: to some degree, at least, the fault for my train wreck of a life must fall upon a condition of which I had no knowledge, hence no control. We can't disentangle in retrospect how much moral culpability I still bear for my own failings; as with most things, the wisest course is to trust in God's Mercy and brace for His Justice.

As you've observed, there's little talk of the martial arts in the above. This is why I brought this memoir to a close at a point in my life when the theme was still immediately relevant; but, as the folks at Mater Media pointed out, I myself would be upset if a spiritual autobiography I was reading left out the ten most recent years.

I was laid off during Covid, and spent the summer of 2020 as a security officer at Leominster Hospital: there I got to air my skills somewhat, when we got a hyper meth-OD off the ambulance or someone rambunctious in the psych ward. And to be sure, I still have black-mood days where I fantasize about someone giving me cause to vent my frustrations into their squishy torso. By and large, however, my fighting days are behind me for the nonce.

Mind you—I've got two daughters, whom I love more than I ever dreamed it was possible to love. You'd better believe I'll be teaching them to kick ass. They'll eat their vegetables, say their prayers, and practice their katas while they're under my roof. The arts will always be a part of who I am.

Ever heard of non-battle battle-anime? It's a sub-sub-genre of Japanese cartooning that uses well-worn kung-fu tropes—a mentor, a nemesis, an escalating round of training and challenges—to tell stories about stuff like swimming or basketball, or even wine-tasting. (Seriously.) In like manner, I still visualize my daily existence as a series of brawls against things like my entropic inclination to stay in bed when it's time yet again to get up and go mop the floors. ("Gae out and bar the door!") And when I need an extra burst of energy, I still close my eyes and imagine going Super-Saiyan. Mock all you like, it works.

I finally *got* Covid this January (2022), and was off my feet for the better part of two months. But as I write these words in April of the same year, I'm working toward being back in training and ready to hold my own once more. Now that I've got kids, I pray for peace and stability instead of battle and adventure; but the Lord don't forget our prayers. I may yet be given what I asked for long ago. If the day comes when we must fight for our Faith, beloved friends, I'll be honored to stand with you. Glory be to God forever!

界

In the middle with brothers
of the Kai

Loosening up to take
out the trash

Posing for the cover

Jumping
for joy at
our wedding
reception

*Ellie and me celebrating
our marriage with Pope Francis*

Made in the USA
Middletown, DE
21 July 2022